When The Mask Slips...

When the Mask Slips... copyright © 2024 by Emma Veilwood. All rights reserved.

No part of this publication may be reproduced, distributed, or transmitted in any form or by any means, including photocopying, recording, or other electronic or mechanical methods, without the prior written permission of the publisher, except in the case of brief quotations embodied in critical reviews and certain other noncommercial uses permitted by copyright law.

This book is a work of non-fiction based on the true experiences of the author. Names, characters, businesses, places, events, locales, and incidents are either the products of the author's memory or used in a fictitious manner. Any resemblance to actual persons, living or dead, or actual events is purely coincidental.

First Edition, 2024

Printed in the United States of America

ISBN: 978-1-7383396-0-0
ISBN Ebook: 978-1-7383396-1-7

When The Mask Slips...

To My [step]Mom:
A Beacon of Guidance

In the tapestry of my life, woven with threads of trial and grace,
Your presence shines—a beacon of unwavering guidance and embrace.
You, who stepped into a story mid-verse,
Taught me the power of love, in the universe.

Through your eyes, I saw a reflection not marred by my past,
But a future bright, possibilities vast.
You showed me compassion without condition,
A gift, beyond measure, beyond tradition.

In moments of darkness, when shadows crept near,
Your light was a promise, dispelling all fear.
You taught me to laugh, to see joy in the rain,
To dance in the storm, to find gain in the pain.

You accepted me, whole, with all my scars and dreams,
In your garden of love, hope blossoms and gleams.
With you, I learned to believe in the morrow,
To embrace life.s tapestry, with its joy and its sorrow.

Trigger Warnings

Please be advised that this book explores themes and contains material that may be triggering or uncomfortable for some readers. Discretion is advised for those with sensitivities to the following topics:

- Depression: Descriptions and explorations of depressive thoughts and feelings.
- Anxiety: Discussions and portrayals of anxiety, including panic attacks and chronic worry.
- Loneliness: Themes of isolation and the emotional impact of feeling alone.
- Self-Worth: Exploration of low self-esteem and struggles with self-image.
- Body Image: Discussions related to body dysmorphia and negative body image.
- Mental Health Struggles: General exploration of mental health issues and their impact on daily living.
- Emotional Abuse: Implicit references to emotional abuse and its psychological effects.
- Fear of Abandonment: Themes revolving around the fear of being left or forsaken.
- Vulnerability: Depictions of emotional vulnerability that may resonate deeply with some readers.
- Suicidal Thoughts: While not explicitly detailed, there may be passing references to thoughts of suicide or self-harm.

If any of these topics might cause distress or trigger unwelcome feelings, please prioritize your mental health and well-being, possibly choosing to read with support or when you feel prepared.

For those who are struggling, remember: you are not alone, and support is available. Don't hesitate to reach out to a mental health professional, a trusted loved one, or a support organization in your community.

Contents

Introduction 7

Chapter One: The Mask of Perfection 9

Chapter Two: Behind the Mask 50

Chapter Three: The Mask Slipping 111

Chapter Four: Without the Mask 177

Conclusion 218

Welcome to "When the Mask Slips...", a collection of poetry that seeks to explore the hidden corridors of the human heart, the silent struggles that we cloak under the guise of normalcy, and the profound journey towards embracing our authentic selves.

In these pages, you will find reflections on loneliness, meditations on self-worth, and confrontations with the shadows of depression and anxiety. This collection is born from personal experience, from the intimate knowledge of what it means to navigate the complex dance of presenting a facade to the world while grappling with the tumultuous sea of emotions within.

Each chapter of this book—The Mask of Perfection, Behind the Mask, The Mask Slipping, and Without the Mask—serves as a milestone on the path towards self-discovery and acceptance. Through the lens of poetry, we will delve into the pressures of conforming to societal expectations, the isolation that can accompany our inner battles, the moments of vulnerability that reveal our true selves, and the liberation found in shedding our masks.

This journey is not just mine; it is ours. It is a call to anyone who has ever felt alone in their struggles, to anyone who has yearned for a sense of belonging, and to anyone who seeks solace in the shared experience of being human. "When the Mask Slips..." is an invitation to witness, to connect, and to find comfort in the understanding that our vulnerabilities do not weaken us; they unite us.

As you turn these pages, I hope you find moments of resonance, passages that speak to your soul, and the reassurance that your feelings are valid. May this collection be a companion on your journey, a reminder that even in our darkest moments, there is light, there is hope, and there is a way forward.

Your mental health matters, and through the act of sharing our stories, we find strength. Thank you for joining me on this journey. Let us walk together, unmasked and unafraid, into the light of acceptance and self-love.

Chapter One:

The Mask of Perfection

Beneath a sky so vast and blue,
A smile that hides the truth from view.
A mask so finely tuned and wrought,
With threads of joy, so falsely caught.

In public's eye, it gleams so bright,
A beacon in the darkest night.
Yet, in the mirror, late at night,
The smile fades to sorrow's plight.

For who can tell, behind those eyes,
The silent battles, hidden cries?
A world of laughter, light, and cheer,
Yet inside, a well of fear.

This mask, a shield from prying gaze,
A fortress in the bustling maze.
Yet, as the stars ascend the sky,
The soul behind the mask asks, "Why?"

Why hide the tears, the pain, the strife?
Why wear a mask through all of life?
Perhaps, in showing our true face,
We'll find our true, our rightful place.

In the dim light, where shadows fall,
Faces flicker, not one but all.
A masquerade of silent cries,
Where truth is masked, and the spirit dies.

No words spoken, no eyes meet,
Just shadows dancing, in deceit.
A wall of smiles, wide and thin,
Hiding the void, the emptiness within.

Each shadow tells a tale untold,
Of dreams turned dust, of hearts grown cold.
Yet in the dance, a desperate plea,
For someone to look, to really see.

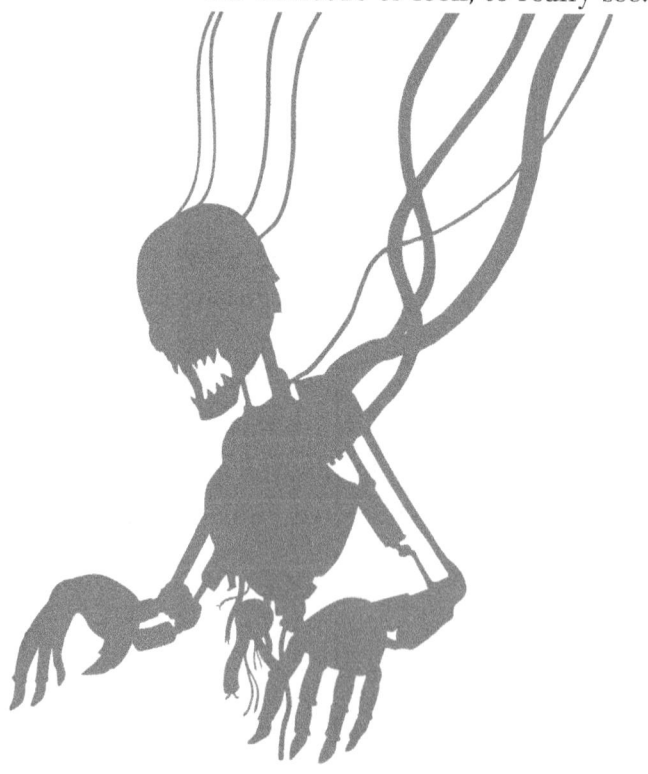

Burdens not seen, but deeply felt,
A deck of cards, expertly dealt.
Expectations, high and mighty,
A silent scream, in the night, flighty.

Heavy, yet weightless, they float around,
A symphony with no sound.
Carrying more than what meets the eye,
Under a weightless sky, a silent cry.

No form, no shape, these specters haunt,
In the garden of dreams, they jaunt.
Yet within, a fire burns bright,
Fighting the shadows, seeking the light.

A mirror stands, tall and grim,
Reflecting a world, so stark and dim.
A figure stares, through glass, through time,
Searching for truth, in a pantomime.

The face that looks back, a stranger's guise,
Behind the glass, a thousand lies.
A smile painted, a laugh contrived,
A soul that wonders, if it's truly alive.

Yet, through the cracks, a light does seep,
A glimmer of hope, buried deep.
For in the reflection, amidst the strife,
Lies the power to forge a life.

On a canvas of silence, emotions are painted,
In strokes bold and colors tainted.
A portrait of solitude, in hues of gray,
Where words are lost, and fears stay.

The brush dips in a well of tears,
Drawing out the unspoken fears.
Each stroke, a whisper, a hidden plea,
A yearning for what could be.

In this gallery of silent screams,
Dreams float, in fractured beams.
Yet, in the quiet, a hope does thrive,
In silent paintings, we find we're alive.

In the quiet before dawn, where thoughts run deep,
A soul wanders, awake in sleep's keep.
Faces worn by day, now rest on the nightstand,
A collection of masks, not quite as planned.

Light filters in, hesitant, breaking through curtains drawn,
Illuminating the edges of facades, worn and torn.
The silence speaks in volumes, a testament to the fight,
Of a spirit battling shadows, away from the light.

Here, in the solitude of the early morn,
Truths whisper softly, in forms unborn.
A gentle reminder of the strength within,
A call to shed the mask, let new chapters begin.

Mirrors, oh mirrors, lined up like silent judges,
Reflecting more than they should, holding grudges.
A face stares back, morphing with the light,
A stranger at times, caught in perpetual twilight.

The eyes, do they show a glimmer of recognition,
Or do they too, partake in the silent omission?
Each glance, a conversation unspoken,
Between the self and its mirrored token.

In this dance of reflection and deflection,
Lies a yearning for connection, a direction.
To see beyond the surface, the superficial,
And embrace the chaos, the beautifully atypical.

There's a war that rages, silent and unseen,
On a battlefield where self-worth and doubt convene.
No clashing of swords, no cries of combat,
Just the quiet struggle, an internal spat.

The mind, a fortress under siege,
Where thoughts like invaders, converge and league.
Barricades built from fears and lies,
Hidden from the world, behind smiling eyes.

Yet, in this solitude, there's a resilience found,
A stubborn hope, in the battleground.
For each battle faced, each day anew,
Is a testament to the strength that grew.

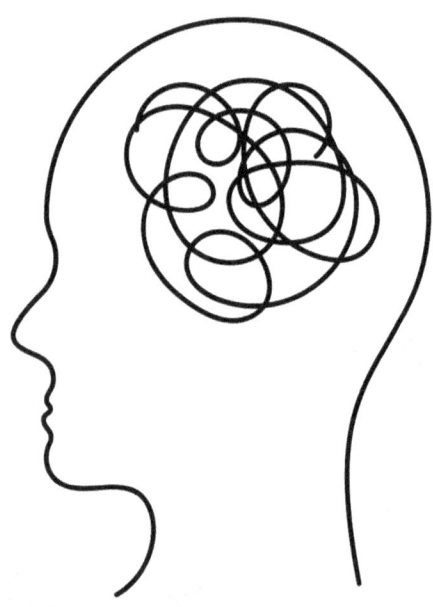

Life, a stage where we dance, perform,
Adhering to norms, trying to conform.
Each step, each move, a calculated art,
In the choreography of pretense, we play our part.

But what of the moments between the acts,
When the lights dim, revealing the facts?
There, in the shadows, truths pirouette,
In a dance of defiance, a silent duet.

The heart beats a rhythm, unique, untaught,
In the quiet, a battle of authenticity fought.
A dance of one's own, in the wings, it awaits,
For the courage to step out, redefine the dictates.

Before the world stirs into its relentless hustle,
there lies a moment suspended in the veil of dawn,
where shadows and light blend,
casting neither judgment nor distinction
upon the faces of those who walk the thin line
between who they are and who they pretend to be.

In this hushed serenity, the mask is neither needed nor missed,
a brief respite where the soul whispers to the waking day
of dreams unmasked, desires unveiled,
and the quiet courage that grows
in the soft light of dawn,
a courage that speaks of hope,
a day when the mask is no longer a shield
but a relic of a battle fought and won.

In the corridor of the self, where echoes walk silently,
bearing the stories of a thousand concealed tears,
there is a space untouched by the light,
where truth resides, quiet and unassuming.

These walls, they listen,
to the silent screams of hearts encaged
by their own fears, their own doubts,
a symphony of silent echoes,
each note a cry for recognition,
for a moment of raw, unfiltered existence.

In this sanctuary of silence,
the echoes speak of a desire to break free,
to live loudly, to love boldly,
to exist without the confines of a mask,
a testament to the strength found
in the silent echoes of our being.

There is an art to the disguise we wear,
a craftsmanship that goes beyond mere facade,
each layer, a stroke of genius or despair,
painted with the brush of societal norms,
coated in the varnish of expectations.

But beneath the surface lies the original canvas,
a masterpiece of complexities,
of light and shadow,
of strokes bold and timid,
a work of art in its own right,
yearning for the day it can be displayed
in the gallery of the world,
unframed, unfiltered,
in its breathtaking, authentic glory.

In between breaths, there is a space,
a momentary lapse where truth and facade collide,
where the mask slips,
and the person between the breaths is revealed,
vulnerable, raw,
a fleeting glimpse into the soul
that dwells within the confines of the constructed self.

It is in these interludes,
these brief pauses in the perpetual performance,
that we find the essence of our true nature,
not in the words spoken
but in the silence that falls between,
a silence that speaks volumes
of fears, hopes, dreams, and the longing
to simply be, unadorned, unmasked,
in the sacred space between breaths.

In the solitude of my mind, a tempest brews,
Words unspoken, forming bruises blues.
A storm of thoughts, too wild to tame,
Each one sharp, calling my name.

I trap them inside, a prisoner to my own guise,
Fearful of the burden, my truth might rise.
So, I smile, a mask so carefully worn,
Hiding a soul, tattered and torn.

It's not your burden to bear, this chaos I host,
So, I swallow the screams, becoming their ghost.
A silent guardian of my own despair,
Pretending it's nothing, just empty air.

Chains, not of steel, but of silence, bind,
Tightening with every truth I find.
To speak would be to shatter the peace,
So, I hold my tongue, and let no word release.

These chains, they're invisible, yet they confine,
Restricting the heart, the soul, the mind.
A burden unshared, a weight unseen,
A life half-lived, somewhere in between.

I carry this load, alone, unaided,
A choice made, the colors faded.
For fear of causing you undue pain,
I remain silent, bound by invisible chains.

In the echo of my silence, a truth untold,
A story of struggle, of warmth turned cold.
I've built a fortress around my heart,
Where my deepest fears lie apart.

It feels unjust, to make you see
The darkest parts that live in me.
So, I lock them away, out of sight,
Into the silence of the endless night.

Yet in this quiet, an echo grows,
A testament to the path I chose.
For in my silence, a strength is found,
A resilience, in the echoes of silence, profound.

Wearing a smile, day by day,
A costume, in which I lose my way.
It feels wrong, this pretense, a lie,
To make believe, not to cry.

I fear to share, to let you in,
On the chaos that lives within.
It's not right, for us both to drown,
In the depths where my fears abound.

So, I carry this facade, a heavy load,
Walking alone, on this winding road.
Hiding the screams, the tears that beg release,
In the burden of pretense, I seek my peace.

With every dawn, I paint my face,
With strokes of strength, in fear's embrace.
A masterpiece of smiles and grace,
Hiding the void, the empty space.

This art of disguise, meticulously refined,
A shield against the world, unkind.
Yet beneath the surface, a soul cries,
Yearning for release, for the disguise to die.

I've become a guardian of secrets, mine alone,
Holding back truths to the world unknown.
Each secret, a weight, a stone in my heart,
A testament to the role I unwillingly impart.

It's a burden I carry, to keep you safe from me,
From the darkness within, that nobody else can see.
So, I tread lightly, softly, maintaining the lie,
That all is well, as I silently sigh.

In the veil of silence, I wrap my pain,
A cloak of quiet, to hide the strain.
Words unspoken, fears untold,
In the silence, my truths unfold.

It's a silent pact I've made, with myself,
To keep my worries, my doubts, on the inner shelf.
For sharing the load, feels too much to ask,
So, in silence, I don my mask.

I walk in the shadows of myself, a specter in the light,
A figure of what could be, if I just might.
But fear holds me back, keeps me hidden,
In the shadows, where my true self is forbidden.

This duality I live, each and every day,
A battle between what I am and what I portray.
A longing to be seen, truly, as I am,
Yet, trapped in the shadows, a perpetual sham.

It's a solitary dance, this life I lead,
Twirling alone, with my unspoken needs.
Each step, each turn, perfected over time,
A rhythm of solitude, a silent chime.

No one sees the falter, the stumble in the dark,
For I dance alone, where my true self embarks.
In this dance, I find my solace, my silent plea,
For a moment of truth, where I can simply be.

Behind the laughter, a tear hides,
A well of sorrow, deep inside.
For every chuckle, every grin,
Is a battle that I do not win.

It's a mask I wear, so well, so bright,
To keep my true feelings out of sight.
But behind the laughter, the facade,
Lies a truth, stark and unclad.

In the quiet, a cost is borne,
A price of silence, heavy and worn.
Each word not spoken, each truth concealed,
In the fabric of my being, forever sealed.

The silence is golden, or so they say,
Yet, in its depths, my colors fade to gray.
A compromise, a sacrifice, a loan,
For the peace of others, my sorrows sown.

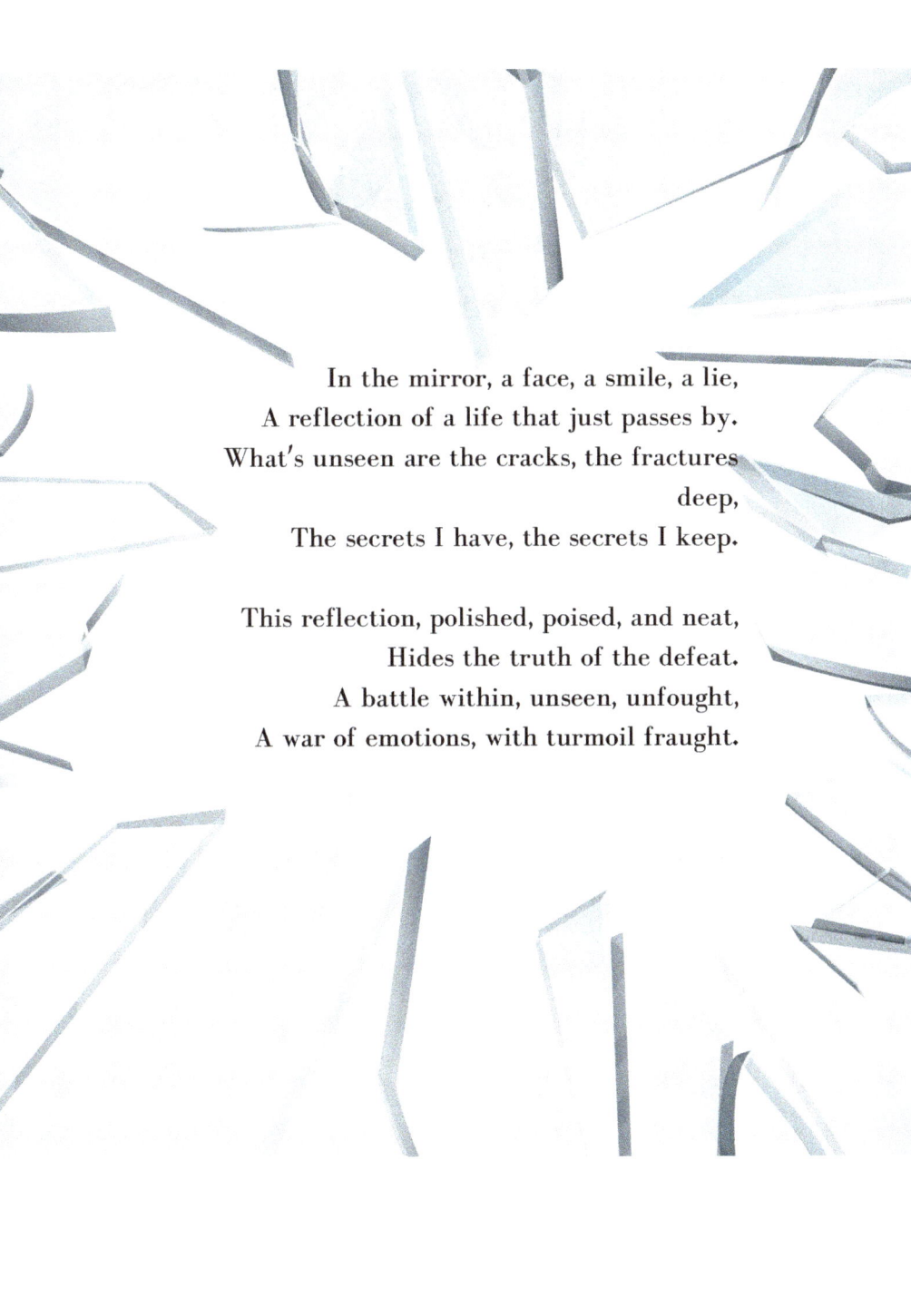

In the mirror, a face, a smile, a lie,
A reflection of a life that just passes by.
What's unseen are the cracks, the fractures deep,
The secrets I have, the secrets I keep.

This reflection, polished, poised, and neat,
Hides the truth of the defeat.
A battle within, unseen, unfought,
A war of emotions, with turmoil fraught.

An echo of a whisper, in the vastness of my soul,
A hint of my truth, trying to take control.
But quickly silenced, quickly stowed away,
For fear of what others might say.

This whisper, though faint, is fierce and true,
A sliver of me I wish I could pursue.
Yet, in the din of life, it fades to naught,
A battle of existence, tirelessly fought.

I don a costume of joy, of glee,
A character far removed from the real me.
This outfit, so bright, so falsely keen,
Covers the darkness, the spaces between.

Each laugh, each jest, a part of the play,
A performance I perfect, day by day.
But beneath the costume, hidden from view,
Lies a soul, yearning to break through.

Underneath the mask, a world untold,
A story of a heart, both warm and cold.
A land of shadows, of light, of dreams,
Where nothing is quite as it seems.

Here, in the depths, the true self resides,
A place where my essence quietly hides.
Wishing for a moment, for a crack in the facade,
For a chance to show the path I've trod.

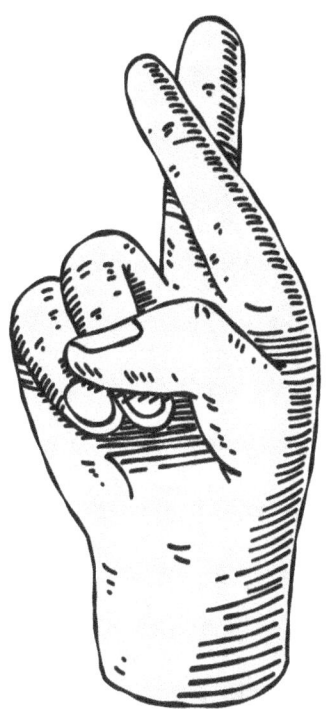

We make a silent pact, you and I,
To look away, to let the truth lie.
I promise to smile, to keep the peace,
To let my inner tumult cease.

This pact, unspoken, yet clear and strong,
Guides our dance, our life, our song.
But within this agreement, a longing still,
For a break in the silence, for the truth to spill.

A lament for the facade, so carefully built,
A structure of smiles, free of guilt.
It stands tall and proud, a monument to fear,
A testament to the things I hold dear.

Yet, within its walls, a soul does weep,
For the truth it cannot keep.
A longing for the day, when the facade can fall,
And the true self can finally stand tall.

An armor of smiles, worn day by day,
A shield against the world, in every way.
Crafted from laughter, from joy feigned,
A fortress, where true feelings are chained.

Yet, beneath the armor, a heart beats wild,
Longing to be seen, not as strong, but as a child.
A soul that dreams of shedding the weight,
Of living a life, unmarred by fate.

There exists a verse, unspoken, unheard,
Filled with the depth of every word.
It lives in the silence, in the space between breaths,
In a realm where truth meets death.

This verse, a melody of the soul's plea,
To be understood, to be set free.
Yet, it remains silent, for fear of the cost,
Of revealing a battle, already lost.

A canvas painted with strokes of pretense,
A masterpiece of avoidance, dense.
Each layer, a lie, a moment deferred,
A picture of happiness, absurd.

Beneath the paint, the canvas weeps,
For authenticity, it silently seeks.
A desire to be seen, in true colors, bright,
Not hidden by layers, out of sight.

In the light, the shadow dances, alone,
A reflection of a self, unknown.
It moves with grace, with poise, with fear,
A silent echo, crystal clear.

This dance, a ritual of the hidden heart,
A performance where shadows play their part.
A longing for the light, to be embraced,
Yet, fearing the truth, it must be faced.

A masquerade ball, within the mind,
Where truths and lies are intertwined.
Each thought, a mask, a disguise,
Hiding the pain from prying eyes.

Yet, in the dance, a step out of line,
A glimpse of the truth, accidentally divine.
A moment of vulnerability, quickly concealed,
In the masquerade of the mind, sealed.

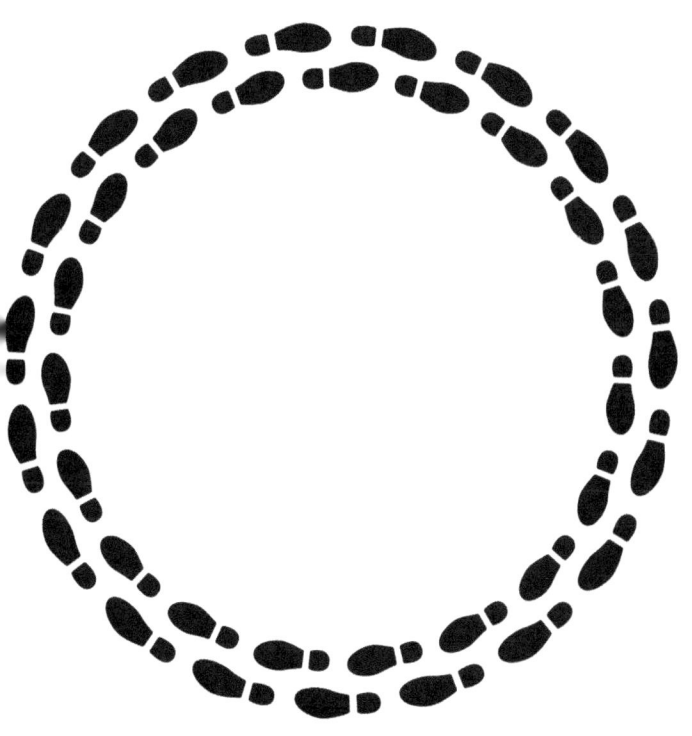

Echoes of the heart, soft and low,
Carry the weight of unspoken woe.
They reverberate in the chambers, deep,
Where secrets and sorrows silently sleep.

These echoes, a reminder of what's at stake,
Of the risk, the fear, the potential heartbreak.
Yet, they also speak of a hope, a desire,
For a connection, true and entire.

This facade takes its toll, day by day,
A price that the soul must pay.
For every smile, every nod, every lie,
A piece of authenticity dies.

Yet, the cost seems a necessary trade,
In a world where judgments are easily made.
A sacrifice for peace, for tranquility,
In the pursuit of societal acceptability.

Behind the curtain of smiles, a play unfolds,
A story of a life, in patterns old.
A narrative of happiness, publicly declared,
While privately, the soul is ensnared.

This play, a production of the highest cost,
Where the true self is lost.
Yet, yearning for a scene, unscripted, real,
Where the heart can truly feel.

The walls whisper, of secrets kept,
Of tears silently wept.
They speak of the burdens, carried alone,
Of the depths of the soul, unknown.

These whispering walls, companions true,
Hold the stories, of the facade's hue.
A testament to the strength, the strife,
Of the hidden layers of life.

Invisible threads, weaving through the day,
Connecting the masks, in a silent ballet.
They bind us together, in pretense, in guise,
In a tapestry of lies.

Yet, these threads also hold the potential,
For a connection, essential.
A hope that beyond the masks, we'll find,
A truth, a bond, of a different kind.

Chapter Two:

Behind The Mask

In the hush of night, in solitude's embrace,
Echoes of my thoughts in endless space.
The crowd's distant murmur, a forgotten song,
Here, in the silence, where I belong.

Walls whisper secrets, in shadows cast,
Of dreams long vanished, in the vast.
The echo of my footsteps, in an empty hall,
A reminder of the times I had the gall.

To dream of light, of love, of laughter loud,
Now, all that's left is solitude's shroud.
Yet, in this quiet, in this isolation keen,
Lies a beauty, in the spaces between.

For in the echoes of my solitary state,
I find a peace, a respite from fate.
A moment to breathe, to simply be,
In solitude's embrace, I find me.

In the stillness of night, whispers in the dark,
Murmurs of a soul's journey, stark.
Loneliness, a constant companion in the shadow,
Walking beside me, in every hollow.

The echo of my steps, a solitary sound,
In the vast emptiness, I am bound.
Depression's grip, tight and unyielding,
A battle fought within, silently wielding.

Yet, in the whispers, a flicker of might,
A soft reminder of the fight.
For even in darkness, a light can grow,
Guiding the way, with a gentle glow.

There's an invisible thread that binds,
Connecting hearts, transcending minds.
Yet, in the depths of despair, it feels frayed,
A lifeline, once strong, now portrayed.

Depression, a thief in the night,
Stealing colors, dimming light.
But even when all seems lost, and hope but a thread,
Remember, it's still there, not gone, not dead.

This invisible thread, woven with care,
A testament to the strength we bear.
A reminder, in times of sorrow and dread,
That we are connected, by an invisible thread.

A chorus of voices, within the void,
Echoes of self, fragmented, annoyed.
Words that sting, with venom, they speak,
A never-ending siege, leaving one weak.

Yet, amid the cacophony, a silence profound,
A space where peace, however fleeting, is found.
A realization dawns, through the din and the doubt,
The strongest voice can be a whisper, not a shout.

In the battle with the voices that bind and berate,
The power to quiet them, to redefine one's fate.
With the last of one's strength, a stand, tall and brave,
A journey from the edge, back from the grave.

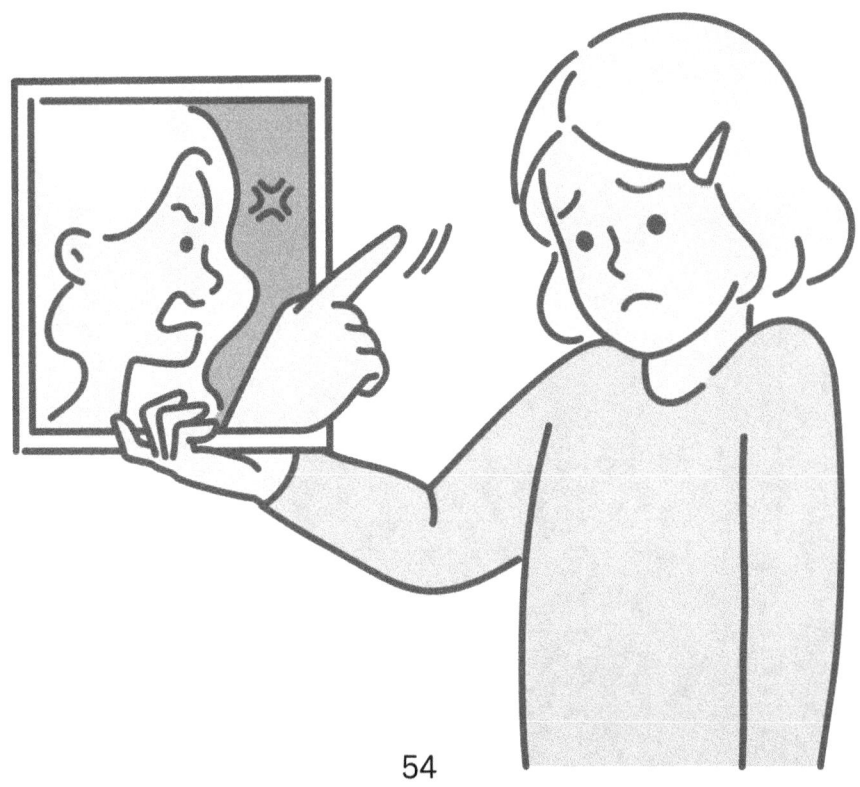

In the dance of shadows and light,
A battle waged out of sight.
The darkness of depression, a heavy shroud,
Silencing the vibrant, the bold, the loud.

Yet, in the deepest shadows, light persists,
A stubborn hope that resists.
For every shadow cast, there is a source,
A light, however faint, on its course.

It's in this interplay of dark and bright,
We find our strength, our will to fight.
A balance sought, between night and day,
In the dance of shadows, we find our way.

Beneath the surface, an armor worn,
Forged in battles, unseen, forlorn.
A shield against the tide of despair,
A defense crafted with utmost care.

Depression's assault, relentless and crude,
Met with a resilience, quiet and shrewd.
For within each of us, lies a warrior's heart,
Ready to fight, to stand apart.

This armor, invisible to the eye,
Is our strength when the night is nigh.
A reminder, in moments of doubt and fear,
That we possess the power to persevere.

Within the silence, battles rage
A war with oneself, across every age
Marks of strife that the world never sees
Hidden scars, a personal decree

A hatred blooms, from seed to tree
For feeling trapped, yearning to be free.
Yet, within the turmoil, a whisper so slight
A flicker of strength, in the depth of night.

The edge of despair, a precipice wide
Yet back from the brink, a step to the side.
For even in darkness, a choice remains
To fight once more, through the pain, the chains.

Staring into the abyss, a reflection stares back,
Eyes full of questions, of all that one lacks.
The urge to self-harm, a storm raging within,
A battle of wills, a fight to begin.

Hating the feeling, yet unable to break free,
A cycle of pain, a desperate plea.
But within the abyss, a spark of light,
A reminder of day, amidst eternal night.

A strength unknown, from depths unseen,
Emerges when hope seems but a dream.
A step away from the edge, a breath taken slow,
A choice to heal, to let the darkness go.

In the quiet aftermath of storms passed,
Echoes of resilience, vast.
A heart weary from battles fought,
With whispers of negativity, fraught.

Yet, in this weariness, a strength untold,
A resolve forged in the fires, bold.
For every voice that speaks in tones so bleak,
There lies a counterpoint, a truth to seek.

A recognition of the struggle, the pain,
And yet a decision to rise again.
In the echoes of resilience, a melody pure,
A song of those who endure.

In the depths of night, where shadows merge with soul,
A darkness that swallows, consuming whole.
Whispers of despair, like tendrils, entwine,
In the absence of light, where no stars align.

A heart echoes in chambers, cold and bare,
Beating a rhythm of habitual scare.
Lost in a labyrinth of thoughts, so bleak,
A voice that screams, yet cannot speak.

This is the realm of the unseen, the untold,
Where pain is a companion, gripping and bold.
Yet in this darkness, a truth remains,
A struggle with shadows, a soul's silent chains.

Trapped in a mind that's both jailer and cell,
A captive of thoughts, an internal hell.
The bars are made of fears, doubts, and lies,
A prison without walls, under open skies.

Each scar, a marker of battles within,
A testament to pain, to suffering, sin.
The fight to break free, a relentless quest,
In a war with oneself, where there's no rest.

Bound by the chains of one's own making,
A soul in turmoil, constantly aching.
Yet within this confinement, a spark of defiance,
A refusal to bow to the darkness in silence.

Surrounded by a sea of my own despair,
Waves of sorrow, too much to bear.
Each breath, a struggle, against the tide,
Fighting to surface, with nowhere to hide.

Drowning in the depths of my own mind,
Seeking solace, but only shadows find.
The darkness envelops, cold and deep,
Pulling down, into the abyss, steep.

Yet even as the light begins to fade,
A flicker of hope, stubbornly stayed.
A reminder that even in the deepest sea,
The will to survive, to break free, can be.

In the quiet of the night, fears whispered loud,
Cloaked in darkness, in solitude's shroud.
Voices that echo, within and without,
Feeding the insecurities, the doubt.

A cacophony of worries, relentless and grim,
A symphony of anxiety, a haunting hymn.
Each note, a reminder of battles unseen,
A melody of struggle, where peace has never been.

In this concert of fears, where darkness reigns,
A search for silence, for release from chains.
Yet within the whispers, a strength is found,
A resilience, in the echoes, profound.

In the brightest light of day,
Shadows stretch, long and gray.
Amidst the laughter and the cheer,
Loneliness whispers, ever near.

No shelter found under the sun,
The shadows and I, become one.
A noonday ghost, unseen, unheard,
In the crowd, yet undisturbed.

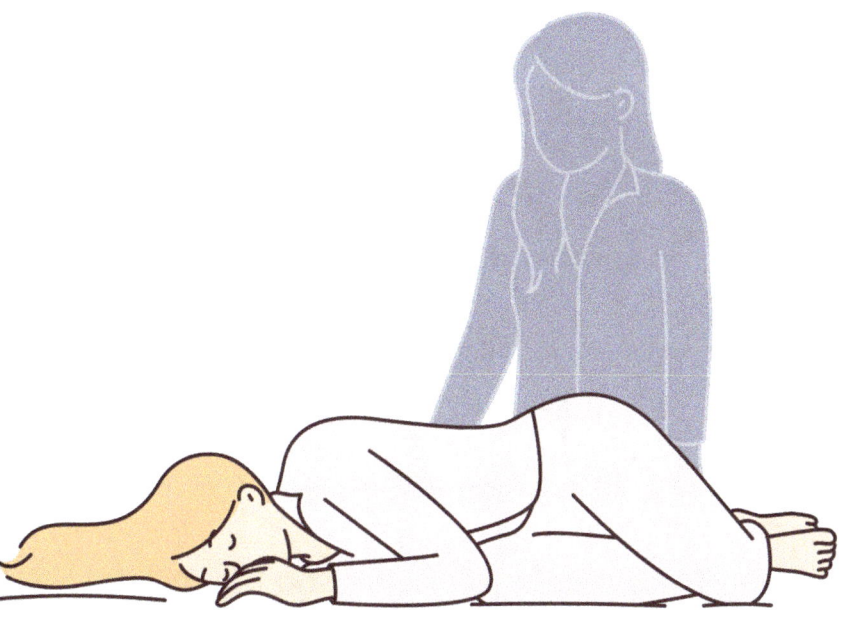

Silent halls within the mind,
Echoes of emptiness, unkind.
A void that speaks in silent screams,
Haunting the remnants of dreams.

In solitude, these echoes grow,
Filling spaces meant to glow.
A resonant void, deep and vast,
Echoes of the present, future, past.

Heavy, the cloak of silence worn,
A burden, silently borne.
Words unspoken, truths untold,
In silence, fears and doubts take hold.

This silence, a weight, unseen,
A barrier to what could have been.
Yet, in its depth, a cry for release,
For words that bring peace.

Beneath the calm, the tides swirl,
Emotions hidden, a secret world.
Invisible currents, pull and push,
A silent storm, a heart's hush.

These tides, unseen, unfelt by others,
Carry the soul, as it flutters.
A quiet struggle, beneath the skin,
Where the battle rages within.

Scattered pieces on the ground,
Fragments of self, lost and found.
Each piece, a story, a memory,
Of what was, and what can never be.

Gathering shards, sharp and true,
Piecing together a semblance of you.
A mosaic of pain and resilience,
A testament to the spirit's brilliance.

An anchor, unseen, holds me fast,
To shadows and whispers, a turbulent past.
Invisible chains, that bind and tether,
Keeping me from drifting, wherever.

This anchor, a burden, heavy and cold,
A silent keeper of stories untold.
Yet, in its grip, a lesson of strength,
Of enduring, of reaching new lengths.

Whispers linger, soft and low,
From the past, a constant echo.
Memories that twist and twine,
Shaping the present, line by line.

These whispers, a reminder, a ghostly spell,
Of lessons learned, of where I fell.
Yet, in their cadence, a path to find,
A way to peace, to leave the past behind.

Behind the curtain of a well-practiced smile,
Lies a battlefield, extending mile after mile.
"Everything's okay," her whispered refrain,
Masking a world of invisible pain.

In solitude's embrace, her truth unfurls,
A silent symphony of chaos whirls.
With every mark, a story untold,
A desperate cry from a soul so bold.

The night whispers secrets in her ear,
Of pain and sorrow, of hidden fear.
Tears mix with blood, in silence, they speak,
Of the strength she seeks, of the peace she seeks.

A smile, a shield, worn day by day,
Hiding the turmoil, keeping the storm at bay.
"I'm fine," she lies, a refrain so bleak,
While inside, her spirit continues to seek.

The quiet of night, her only witness,
To the scars of her battle, her moment of weakness.
A canvas of skin, etched with her pain,
A desperate attempt to feel, to regain.

Her eyes, windows to a storm-raged soul,
Bearing the burden, paying the toll.
A silent scream, for someone to see,
The depth of her pain, her desperate plea.

In the grey dawn of unspoken fears,
Lies a battleground, silent, yet clear.
A war waged between the urge to hide,
And the storm of anxiety, looming wide.

Depression, a blanket heavy and smothering,
Under its weight, the soul quietly suffering.
Each breath, a labor; each moment, a fight,
To find a reason to rise, to seek the light.

Yet, in the stillness, a whisper sharp as steel,
Anxiety's voice, relentless, refusing to kneel.
It speaks of abandonment, of a fate so bleak,
Should the strength to move, to face the day, prove weak.

"Get up, get up," it hisses, a taunt, a jeer,
Preying on the deepest, most primal fear.
That inaction will lead to isolation, a loss so profound,
A world where love and warmth can no longer be found.

Caught in this torment, between stillness and storm,
A spirit battles, worn and torn.
Feeling worthless, yet fearing more the cost of standing still,
A paradoxical prison, crafted from one's own will.

...Continues...

...Continued...

Yet even here, in the depths of despair,
A flicker of defiance, a gasp of air.
For within the heart, a quiet strength does dwell,
A resolve to fight, to rise, to quell.

The battle rages, day by day,
A journey through the grey.
Yet each small victory, each step, each breath,
Is a defiance of the shadows, a challenge to death.

In the space between stillness and storm,
A resilience begins to form.
A recognition that worth is not defined by fear,
And in the fight itself, there is a love so dear.

She walks in daylight, a ghost among shadows,
Her laughter, a mask, concealing her sorrows.
"I'm okay," she whispers, to those who don't see
The wounds she inflicts, just to be free.

In the solitude of her own despair,
She battles demons, gasping for air.
Each scar, a testament to her fight,
Each drop of blood, a flicker of light.

She yearns for a hand, for someone to hold,
To see beyond the facade, the exterior cold.
For someone to notice, to really care,
To acknowledge the pain she can no longer bear.

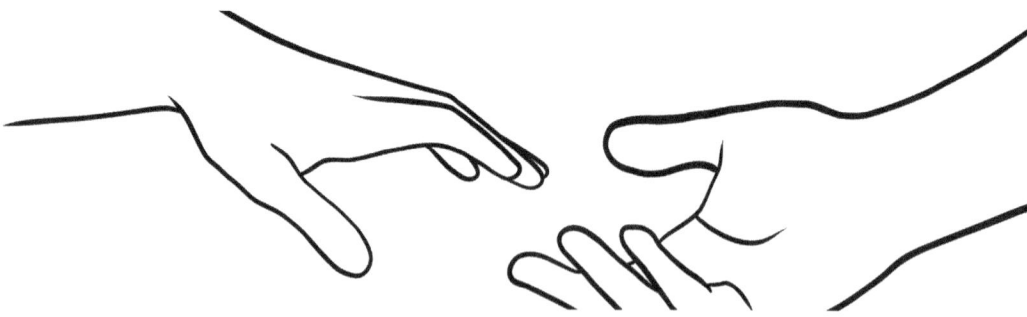

In her silence, a story unfolds,
Of a heart heavy, a soul that holds.
A mask of joy, so bright, so fine,
Veiling a truth, a decline.

The night knows her true face,
Reflecting a heart, lost in space.
Her skin, a canvas of her plight,
Each line a bearer of her fight.

She craves a gaze that truly sees,
Beyond the surface, with ease.
To understand her silent cries,
To soothe her soul, before it dies.

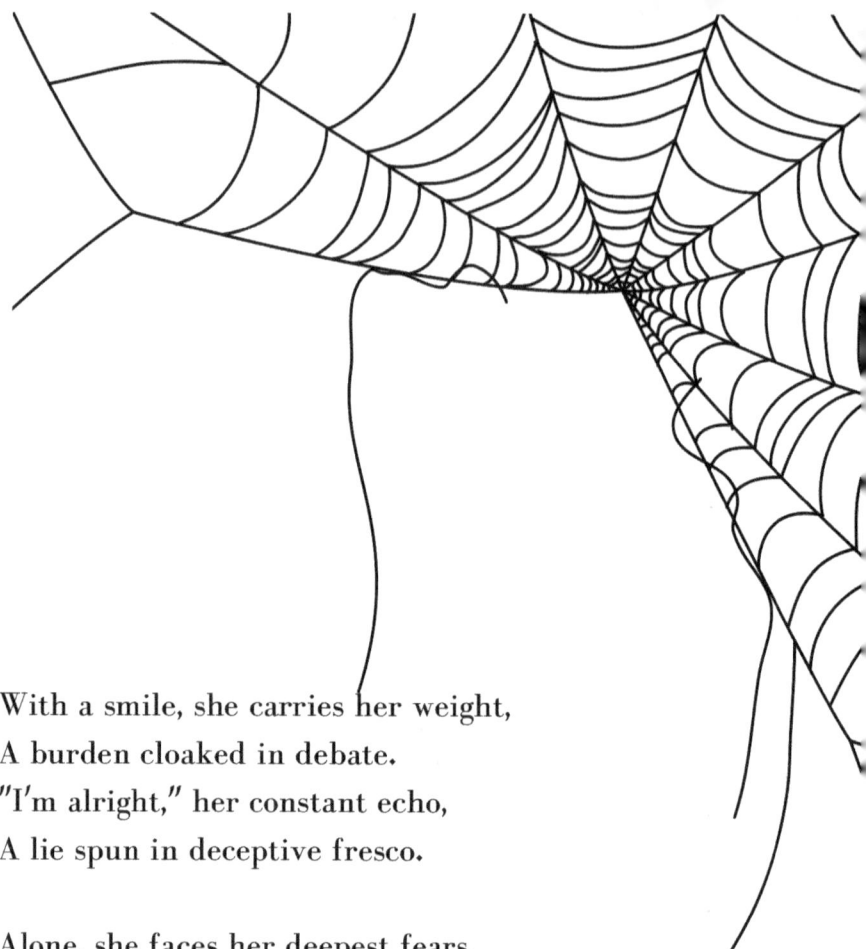

With a smile, she carries her weight,
A burden cloaked in debate.
"I'm alright," her constant echo,
A lie spun in deceptive fresco.

Alone, she faces her deepest fears,
Her canvas streaked with blood and tears.
A silent battle, waged in the night,
A struggle to find the light.

Her scars, a map of her journey,
A call for someone to see, truly.
Each mark, each tear, a silent plea,
For someone to share her agony.

A fortress built to last through storms,
Yet, within, a heart that mourns.
Armor cracks, barely seen,
Reveal a soul, raw, keen.

Through these fissures, light dares creep,
Waking dreams once thought asleep.
In vulnerability, strength we find,
A path to peace, to unwind.

Standing on the edge of dawn,
A new day, yet the same forlorn.
A cycle of hope and despair,
In the soft morning air.

Gazing into fragments scattered,
A self-image, torn and tattered.
In each shard, a different angle,
A psyche, complex, entangled.

Yet within this broken view,
Lies a chance to start anew.
To piece together a truer reflection,
Embracing flaws, seeking connection.

With shadows, a dance, delicate, fine,
A movement between darkness and the divine.
Each step, a balance, a trying feat,
To the rhythm of a heart's discreet beat.

In this dance, a story told,
Of battles brave, of spirits bold.
A dance with shadows, within the soul,
Toward a light, making whole.

On silent fields, the heart does roam,
Fighting battles, far from home.
Quiet wars, within, rage,
A silent storm, from stage to stage.

Each victory, silent, sweet,
Each defeat, a hasty retreat.
Yet, in this quiet, strength is born,
In battles fought, a soul reborn.

A curtain drawn, a smile wide,
Hiding the tumult that resides inside.
Behind the cheer, a silent scream,
A soul adrift, caught in between.

Yet, this curtain, thin as air,
Holds a truth, raw, bare.
That behind the smiles, we all seek,
A bond, a love, a peak.

Dancing with my shadows, a silent ballet,
In a world where light seldom stays.
Each movement, a reflection of pain,
A rhythm of a heart, stained.

These walls, they whisper, secrets deep,
Of the nights with no sleep.
They hold the tales of tears shed,
Of silent prayers, of dread.

But in their whispers, a melody true,
Of resilience, of making through.
A story of triumph, softly spoken,
Of a spirit, unbowed, unbroken.

Invisible threads, pull and weave,
A tapestry of what we believe.
Ties that bind, seen only by the heart,
Holding us together, while apart.

These threads, a network, vast, unseen,
Connect the spaces where we've been.
A reminder, in our silent dread,
We're woven together, by threads unsaid.

A critic resides within, harsh and severe,
Feeding on remnants of old fear.
Every action, every word, dissected,
By a heart, long ago, rejected.

This internal voice, relentless and keen,
Casting shadows on every scene.
Telling me I'm not enough, never will be,
A prisoner of past words, never free.

How do I silence this critic, so cruel,
And rewrite the narrative, as my tool?
To live not in shadows, but in light,
Embracing the day, dispelling the night.

Echoes of the heart, a distant drum,
A reminder of where we've come from.
They speak in rhythms, soft and clear,
Of love, of loss, of all we hold dear.

In these echoes, a resonance found,
A common ground, a shared bound.
A heart's echo, in the silent night,
Brings us together, in the shared light.

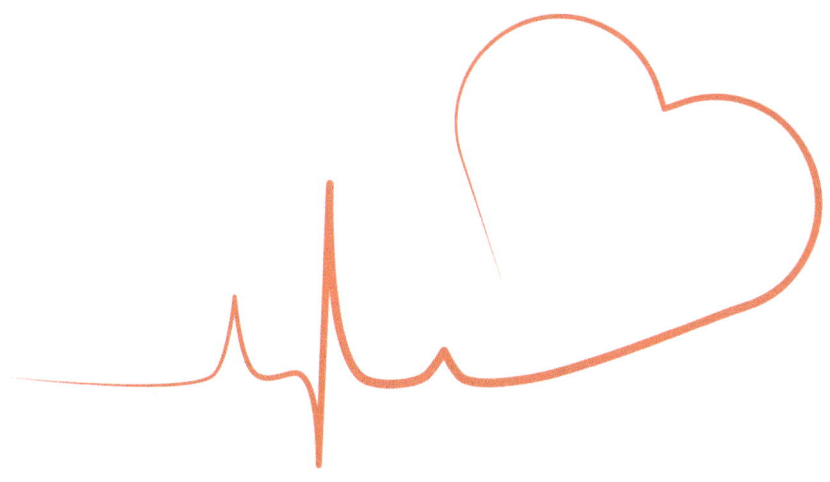

Voices of yesterday, linger and leer,
In moments of quiet, they draw near.
Telling me I'm still that child, small and meek,
Whose voice was stifled, unable to speak.

Every challenge, a mountain steep,
Every valley, a chasm deep.
Haunted by a past that clings and clutches,
A heart that beats, but barely touches.

Yet, in this struggle, a glimmer of hope,
A strength to climb, a way to cope.
For in my voice, a power anew,
To silence the past, to start true.

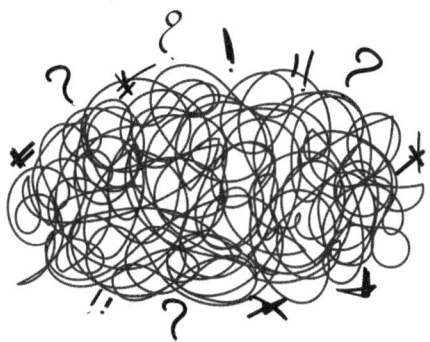

In the quiet, a shadow whispers, cold and sly,
Repeating words that made me cry.
"Never enough," it hisses, a haunting refrain,
A chorus of past pain, again and again.

No matter the effort, the time, the care,
The shadow looms, always there.
A specter of critique, of scorn, of doubt,
Echoing every fear, every shout.

Though years have passed, the voice remains,
A cruel reminder of invisible chains.
Each achievement overshadowed by this curse,
Feeling forever inadequate, or worse.

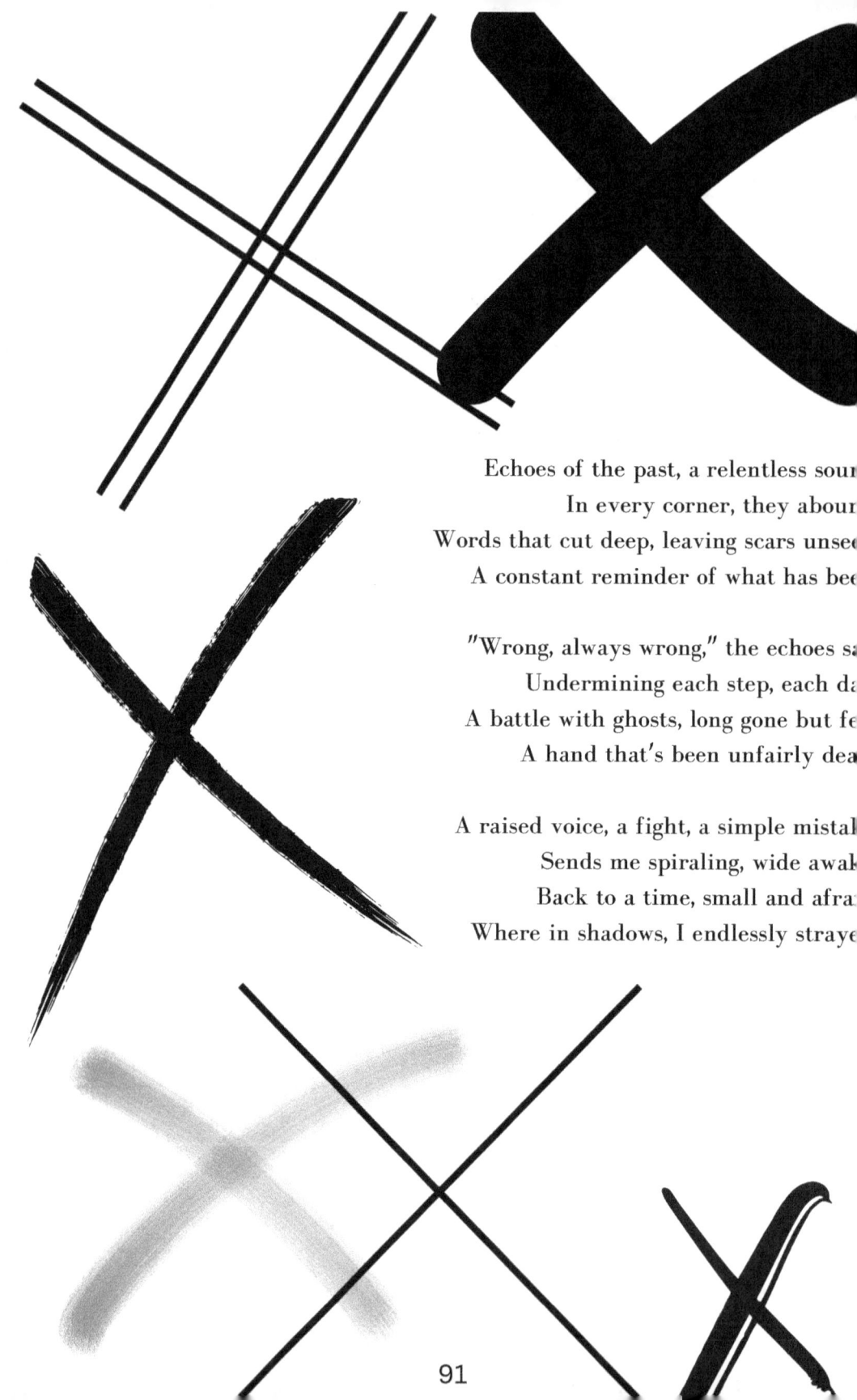

Echoes of the past, a relentless sou[nd]
In every corner, they abou[nd]
Words that cut deep, leaving scars unsee[n]
A constant reminder of what has bee[n]

"Wrong, always wrong," the echoes s[ay]
Undermining each step, each d[ay]
A battle with ghosts, long gone but fe[lt]
A hand that's been unfairly dea[lt]

A raised voice, a fight, a simple mista[ke]
Sends me spiraling, wide awa[ke]
Back to a time, small and afra[id]
Where in shadows, I endlessly straye[d]

Words, once spoken, become a legacy,
Crafting a reality, only I can see.
Told I was too much, or not enough,
Navigating life became unduly tough.

Each achievement, tainted by doubt,
Wondering what critique it's about.
A life lived under the weight of these words,
A flightless bird, among soaring birds.

But within this cage, a key exists,
In new words, in sunlit mists.
A chance to break free, to finally soar,
To live a life where I am no more ignored.

Within the silence of my room,
Echoes of solitude loom.
A whispering void, so vast, so deep,
Where my unspoken sorrows seep.

Carrying a weight unseen,
On shoulders bent, where light's been.
A burden of thoughts, heavy and grim,
A battle fought within, to sink or swim.

Life in shades of grey, no color in sight,
A world dimmed, devoid of light.
Seeking a rainbow in a sky so bleak,
A sign of hope, a streak.

My voice, a whisper against the storm,
Unheard, as if it never was born.
A plea for help, lost in the wind,
An echo of a battle, pinned.

Chains of thought that bind and gag,
A mind's prison, a relentless drag.
Seeking freedom, a break from strife,
A moment's peace in a turbulent life.

In the night's embrace, I find my fears,
Companions of old, through the years.
A solace in stars, a whisper in the moon,
A hope that dawn will break, soon.

Raindrops mirror my silent scream,
A reflection of a broken dream.
In each drop, a story untold,
A piece of my heart, bold yet cold.

The walls whisper secrets of my mind,
A narrative, twisted and entwined.
Seeking solace in a space so confined,
Where echoes of my past are enshrined.

Beneath the calm surface, a storm rages,
A war of emotions, across the ages.
Hidden depths, so dark and wide,
Where my true self resides.

Chasing the fading light of day,
Hoping the darkness might stay away.
Yet, in the twilight, truth becomes clear,
In the fading light, I face my fear.

Echoes of me in an empty room,
A presence felt in the gloom.
A reminder of who I used to be,
Before the world took pieces of me.

A slight crack in the mask I wear,
A glimpse of the truth I bear.
Fearful of what the break might mean,
In a world where only masks are seen.

A tear in the fabric of my soul,
Where the essence of me used to roll.
A patchwork of pain and resilience,
Marking a journey of persistence.

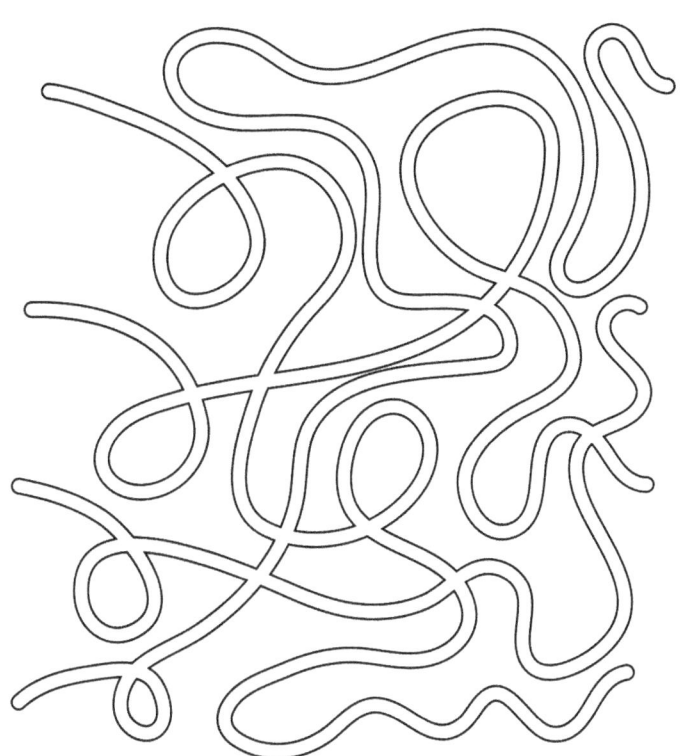

Lost in the labyrinth of my mind,
A way out, I seek but cannot find.
Each thought, a path that twists and turns,
A lesson in the labyrinth, one learns.

In the quiet before the storm,
A sense of dread, a form.
The calm, a deceptive embrace,
Before the storm reveals its face.

Ripples in the pond of my thoughts,
Disturbances from battles fought.
Each ripple, a memory, a moment in time,
A reflection of a mountain I climb.

The wind sighs, a lament for the lost,
A chorus for the frost.
In its breath, a story of strife,
A testament to the fight for life.

In the breaking dawn, a sliver of hope,
A strength to climb, to cope.
The first light, a promise made,
In the breaking dawn, shadows fade.

Chapter Three:

The Mask Slipping

There comes a time, a fleeting glance,
When the mask slips, by happenstance.
A crack in the armor, so carefully worn,
Reveals a soul, tattered and torn.

A laugh too loud, a tear that falls,
A moment of truth, when destiny calls.
The facade crumbles, piece by piece,
Releasing fears, in sudden release.

In that instant, the world sees true,
The person I hid, from view to view.
Vulnerable, raw, exposed to light,
A soul in battle, a warrior in fight.

Yet, in the crack, a beacon shines,
A glimpse of hope, in trying times.
For in vulnerability, there lies a power,
A strength, a courage, in the darkest hour.

So let the mask slip, let the cracks show,
For it's through these fissures, we truly grow.
A soul unveiled, in purest form,
In cracks and crevices, we are reborn.

At the crossroads of concealment and the open heart,
Lies the moment of truth, a fresh start.
The fear of unveiling, layer by layer,
The essence of oneself, laid bare.

The pivotal choice, to hide or reveal,
With the potential to hurt, to heal.
The uncertainty of acceptance, of being seen,
Of letting go of who we've been.

Yet, in this moment, there's a chance for grace,
For connection, in the shared space.
A leap of faith, in the unknown,
Where the seeds of true intimacy are sown.

In the silence of our deepest nights,
Where shadows dwell and fear ignites.
There lies a truth, so often hidden,
Of fears unspoken, forbidden, bidden.

We mask our dread, our deepest qualms,
In the quiet, beneath the palms.
Yet, beneath the surface, it simmers, waits,
A prisoner of our self-made gates.

Words unuttered, thoughts confined,
In the maze of the mind, they intertwine.
Fear of rejection, of being alone,
Of the unknown depths, to us shown.

Yet, sharing our fears, though it seems daunting,
Can turn those haunted nights into morning.
For in the sharing, we find we're not alone,
In our fears unspoken, we've all grown.

In the dance of connections, so intricate and fine,
Lies the fear of the bond's decline.
Fragile threads, woven tight,
In the fear of day, in the dread of night.

The anxiety of a word, a look, a tone,
That could unravel what we've known.
The delicate balance of trust and fear,
Wondering if the end is near.

Yet, in this fragility, there's a beauty so rare,
In the moments we choose to care.
For though the bonds may seem weak,
In their strength, we find what we seek.

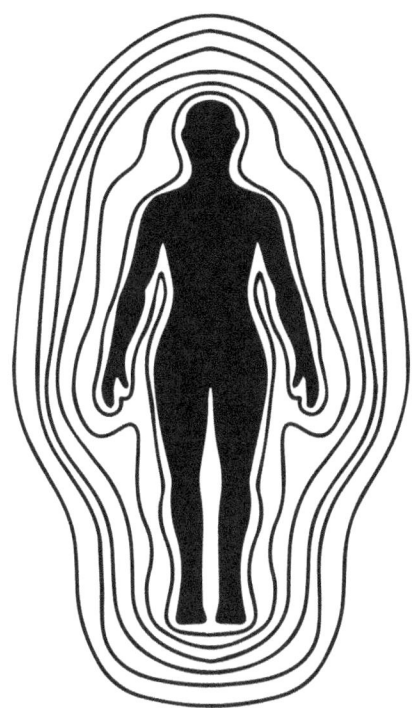

Beneath the guise of smiles and nods,
A soul stirs, with odds at odds.
Vulnerability, a naked flame,
Illuminates the heart's true name.

Exposed, the layers peel away,
Revealing hues of night and day.
Anxiety claws with sharp embrace,
At the thought of showing an honest face.

On the brink of revelation, I stand,
A precipice wrought by my own hand.
The anxiety of exposure, a bitter pill,
Swallowed in the hope of a thrill.

The fear of rejection, a shadow vast,
Tethered to the specters of the past.
Yet, in this vulnerability, a truth so keen,
In the raw and real, I am seen.

To be known, truly, with all my scars,
Is to open locked and rusted bars.
The risk of intimacy, a daunting leap,
Into depths where secrets seep.

But in this risk, a liberation found,
On sacred ground, a truth profound.
Fear of rejection, a ghost that fades,
In the light of connections newly made.

In the crumble of walls, a figure stands,
Not shaped by others' demands.
Embracing authenticity, a power untold,
More precious than silver, more lasting than gold.

The liberation in being simply me,
Unfettered, unmasked, finally free.
To live out loud, in color and song,
In a place where I truly belong.

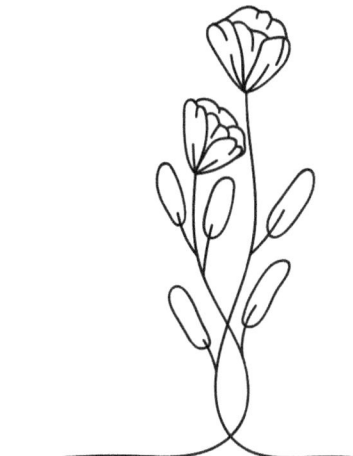

As the mask slips, a soul breathes,
In the space where honesty weaves.
Healing in the open, in the light of day,
Where shadows and doubts may fade away.

In the telling, a strength we find,
A peace of mind, a bind unbind.
For in the act of letting go,
We embrace ourselves, and in doing, grow.

In the mirror of my mind, shadows play,
Reflecting doubts that stalk my day.
A questioning of worth, silent and deep,
A relentless whisper that disturbs my sleep.

Anxiety, a constant, unwelcome guest,
Feeding on fears, never at rest.
Fear of abandonment, a chasm wide,
Where echoes of loneliness keenly reside.

Beneath the scrutiny of unseen eyes,
A soul crumbles, adorned in disguise.
Poor body image, a cage of despair,
A war with oneself, unfair to bear.

Each glance, a judgment, each thought, a blade,
In the battle of perception, endlessly played.
Anxiety, the armor that wears thin,
Against the barrage of what might have been.

In the silence, the fear of leaving,
A heart held hostage, barely breathing.
Abandonment, a ghost that haunts,
In every shadow, in every taunt.

A tether to the fear of being alone,
A bond forged in the unknown.
Yet, in this desolation, a whisper soft,
A reminder of worth, held aloft.

Doubt weaves its chains with cunning art,
Binding the mind, constricting the heart.
Self-worth questioned at every turn,
In the flames of fear, we slowly burn.

Yet, within the ashes, a spark remains,
A defiance against these intangible chains.
For even in moments of despair,
Lies the power to repair.

In the struggle with the image I see,
A journey to accept, to let myself be.
Poor body image, a foe, a test,
In the quest for peace, for a moment's rest.

Yet, in this battle, a realization dawns,
Of beauty not seen, but felt in songs.
A body not just of flaws to lament,
But a vessel of life, uniquely meant.

Shattered silence,
A mirror cracked with despair,
Echoes of self, scattered, bare.
Neglect,
Her only gift received,
Edging further away,
With every breath she believed.

Her pleas,
Mere whispers against the storm,
No anchor to keep him warm.
In her reflection, emptiness she sees,
From the instant he turns,
She's adrift in seas,
Of worthlessness, heavy,
A burden she bears,
In the quiet, where nobody hears.

It creeps in, silent, stealthy, unseen.
Whisper-soft, at dawn.
Gentle, a trickle, a shadow.
I blame the chaos of days, I push through.
It spreads,
Fears, doubts.
Quietly,
For a while,
Steps light,
Murmurs, sighs.
"It.s just for now". I hope, "It will pass".
I march on.
It takes root,
Making itself at home.
Volume rising,
Ever louder.
Echoing anxieties,
Sleepless nights.
"Not again". I plead.
I trudge through my routines.
It grips tight, malicious.
Yelling,
Endless.
Guilt, insignificance, pain.
"Please, leave".
I struggle to stay afloat.
Digging deeper,
Into my soul, my essence.
Flourishing agony,
With each pulse.
Void, isolation,
Forsaken.
Quiet, motionless,
"I.m stuck, I.m lost".

Behind a door that locked away fear,
A confrontation, stark and clear.
Voices raised in a cacophony of pain,
A bond once cherished, now a stain.
The courage it took to stand, to fight,
Against the darkness of that night.

A moment.s terror, a knife.s cold gleam,
A nightmare waking from a dream.
A jacket torn, a symbol, a sign,
Of a line crossed, unforgivable, malign.
Yet, from this abyss, a phoenix's rise,
A will to escape, to sever ties.

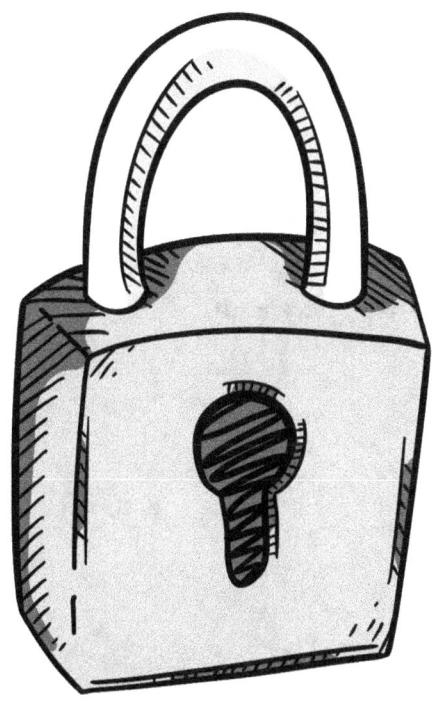

Last night, an old ghost visited,
Gripping my heart with a familiar fear.
Breath stolen by the tightest knot,
Tears mingled with a desperate plea.

It whispered lies of solace in pain,
A false promise of peace in its grasp.
A moment of escape, it claimed to give,
From the storm inside that raged.

But in the wake of its cold caress,
A silence, heavy, filled the air.
Hidden beneath the cloth of day,
A secret borne with deepest care.

Let this not be a burden carried alone,
In shadows where silent battles are fought.
There's strength in reaching for a hand,
In sharing the weight of a troubled thought.

Remember, it's okay to seek the light,
To find a voice in the presence of night.
For in the sharing, healing may start,
And from the ashes, hope may ignite.

My reflection, a fragmented foe,
Distorts the truths I wish to know.
Every curve, each line it twists,
A cruel illusion that persists.

The mirror, a thief of joy,
Turns self-love into its toy.
A knot of anguish, tightly wound,
In its gaze, I am bound.

I search for smiles, for light within,
Against the pull of shadow's din.
A battle to mend, to find release,
From the chains of shame, a quest for peace.

The feeling, raw, beyond words. reach,
A silent scream, a desperate beseech.
Would there were a measure, a means to compare,
This inner turmoil, a burden I bear.

In the mirror.s eye, a distorted view,
A self-perception askew.
It lies, deceives, with every glance,
Stealing away every chance.

My smile, anchored by unseen weights,
Battles with a fate it hates.
I strive to change, to find some solace,
In a world where my mind finds no palace.

Emotions deep, a tumultuous sea,
Crashing waves of what I see.
A longing for a reflection true,
Not this image, skewed in hue.

A search for something, a parallel,
In which my true self might dwell.
Yet in this journey, I hope to find,
A peace for both heart and mind.

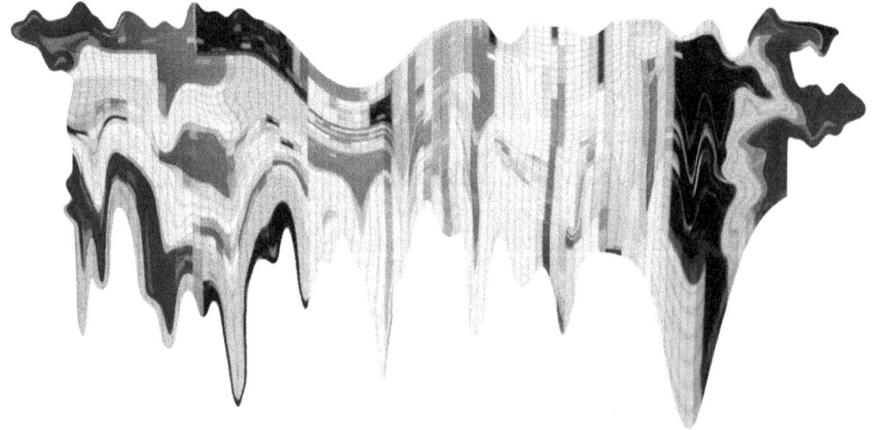

The mirror, a cruel conspirator,
Reflects a story, a distorted narrator.
With every glimpse, it steals a bit more,
Of the happiness from my core.

The corners of my mouth, drawn down,
In its surface, I fear I.ll drown.
I seek to heal, to repair the breach,
For a self-love that seems out of reach.

Feelings, intense, hard to articulate,
A struggle with an unseen opponent I debate.
Oh, for a comparison, a relatable tale,
In which my own narrative might prevail.

Why do my intentions get lost in the air?
Why does my heart feel so stripped and bare?
I try to spread kindness, to make things right,
Yet all I seem to bring is a never-ending night.

I distance myself, a reflex, it seems,
Wrestling with shadows, chasing dreams.
Why has love become a fortress I can't breach?
My own soul's embrace, forever out of reach.

Told to embrace the essence of who I am,
Yet faced with moulds and a societal sham.
Those who preached individuality and grace,
Turned cold shoulders, an about-face.

Now I stand, gazing at a future so bleak,
Feeling so powerless, so fragile, so weak.
If I can't find worth in the mirror's gaze,
How can I navigate this life's maze?

What's inherently lacking within my soul?
Why does every attempt not to hurt just take its toll?
I aim for light, yet darkness is all I seem to sow,
In this garden of life, nothing good does grow.

I push the world away, a defense, a shield,
In the battlefield of love, I'm forced to yield.
How did I become a creature so unlovable, so scorned?
In the quest for acceptance, my heart has worn.

Raised to be me, yet me was never right,
Shaped and trimmed like a bonsai, a pitiful sight.
I've come to understand, through every tear, every bleed,
I'll never be enough, a soul lost to its own creed.

For how can I expect to be cherished and loved,
When my own essence, my core, I've shoved?
Not enough for the world, a truth so bitter,
In this internal war, I'm but a quitter.

What flaw in me makes me so hard to comprehend?
Why do my efforts to belong only offend?
Intentions pure, yet the outcomes are so flawed,
Seeking to heal, yet more wounds are gored.

Retreating into myself, a spiral of doubt,
Wondering what this life's all about.
Once told my heart was gold, my spirit bright,
Now, it feels like I'm lost to the night.

Urged to be authentic, to proudly stand tall,
Yet every step forward precedes a fall.
Moulded by hands that promised to understand,
Left feeling like an outcast in my own land.

Acknowledging the truth is a pill so hard to swallow,
In my own inadequacy, I wallow.
How can I contribute to the world's grand tapestry,
When I'm grappling with being enough, even just for me?

In the halls of memory, their voices still roam,
Cruel taunts that once felt like home.
"Never good enough," they whispered, loud and clear,
A chorus of bullies, year after year.

Their words, like ghosts, in the corners of my mind,
A constant reminder of the ties that bind.
"Always worthless," they echo, a haunting refrain,
In the quiet moments, a familiar pain.

Despite the distance, the years in between,
Their shadows linger, unseen but keen.
A past full of bullies, a memory lane soiled,
Where self-esteem was trampled and toiled.

Their laughter haunts me, a sinister sound,
In the echoes of my mind, it.s bound.
"You'll never amount to anything," they said,
A statement that fills me with dread.

It's the soundtrack of my doubts, playing on repeat,
A melody of insecurities, bitter and sweet.
"Always a loser," they chant, a cruel jest,
Undermining my efforts to do my best.

These voices from the past, a chorus so grim,
Remind me of a time when hope was dim.
They promised I'd be haunted forever,
By words designed to sever.

The shadows whisper, remnants of those days,
When bullies clouded my youthful ways.
Telling tales of a worth so fleeting,
A heart heavy with their relentless beating.

"Useless," they muttered, a verdict so cold,
In the fabric of my soul, it took hold.
Their judgments, like specters, ever present,
A reminder of a time unpleasant.

Yet, in the struggle, a strength was born,
From the very words that meant to scorn.
Though they aimed to tether me to fear,
It's the resilience in their echo I choose to hear.

Though the past is littered with words that wound,
In their midst, a stronger self was found.
For every "worthless" thrown my way,
A step was taken, come what may.

The bullies of yesteryear, architects of doubt,
Unwittingly taught me what strength is about.
Their echoes, once a cage, now a stage,
On which I write my story, page by page.

No longer a prisoner of their cruel game,
I rise above, no longer the same.
For in the whispers of my past's disdain,
I found my voice, my worth, my refrain.

That night, the stars went dark, a void where light once danced,
In his realm, shadows played, where fate by chance was glanced.
A youth misled by whispers sweet, into a lion's den,
Where trust was twisted, boundaries crossed, in the lion's pen.

A door locked, a world collapsed, under a tyrant's whim,
His words like venom, actions vile, on whims both cruel and grim.
The battle cries of a soul ensnared, in terror's tight embrace,
Echoed in a hollow home, a supposed safe space.

With spirits dulled by poison's kiss, his threats like chains did bind,
A desperate plea to the night, for a peace she couldn't find.
A knife, a threat, a moment frozen, in the shadow of despair,
A jacket torn, a symbol marked, by the predator's lair.

Abandoned, when the voices needed to rise as one,
Found solace in a café's laugh, their night of fear undone.
Alone she stood, against the storm, a warrior painted in fright,
Fighting for a dawn's relief, in the longest night.

The aftermath, a silent scream, in the halls of justice, lost,
A narrative dismissed, a cost untold, an unbearable frost.
Yet, in the telling of this tale, a strength from ashes rose,
A phoenix clad in resilience, adorned in battle's prose.

This journey through the darkest night, a testament to her might,
A declaration loud and clear, from the shadows into light.
For though the stars once hid their face, in her heart, a new day's start,
A beacon for the broken, a masterpiece of art.

In breaking silence, chains dissolve, from the grip of terror's night,
Emerging from the shadows, a soul takes flight.
A narrative of pain, of survival, a story boldly told,
A reminder of the strength within, a spirit brave and bold.

In the chill of December's embrace,
A heart was lost, a soul misplaced.
Christmas lights, once bright with joy,
Now reminders of a cruel ploy.

A shadow cast over festive cheer,
Echoes of a past, too painful, too near.
A season of love, turned to fear,
By actions unforgivable, crystal clear.

Yet in the depth of winter's cold,
A spirit brave, a heart bold.
Refusing to let darkness define,
The beauty of the yuletide shine.

Behind the facade of holiday glee,
Lies a tale of agony, unseen.
A warrior fights with silent cries,
Beneath the festive, starlit skies.

Each Christmas carol, a piercing note,
On memories dark, the mind does dote.
Yet, within the battle's fierce embrace,
Lies a strength, a subtle grace.

For though the season brings to mind,
A past best left far behind,
There emerges, from the night,
A will to live, to fight, to write.

In the heart of night's embrace,
Where shadows mocked the light's grace,
A room became a stage for fear,
A script written with a tear.

The door's click, a chilling sound,
A heart's beat, the only other found.
His breath, tainted with vice,
Eyes cold as ice, rolled the dice.

Words slurred, a venomous drip,
Promises of love, a tightening grip.
"No," a whisper lost in the storm,
A refusal met with form.

A struggle, a desperate plea,
A soul's cry to be free.
The sharp threat of a blade.s kiss,
Marking the jacket, a miss.

Trapped in a maze with no end,
Betrayal by those she'd called friend.
Laughter in a cafe, a stark contrast,
To a spirit, broken, harassed.

The aftermath, a world indifferent,
Justice, an illusion, inefficient.
Her word against the void, dismissed,
A wound, a tear, unmissed.

...Continues...

...Continued...

Yet, in this darkest hour, a light,
A strength found in the night.
A voice rising from the silence,
Breaking free from compliance.

This journey, raw, a testament true,
Of a survivor, through and through.
A tale of nights stolen, but also of dawn,
Of a phoenix, reborn, and drawn.

Voices silenced, stories untold,
In the eyes of justice, a cold hold.
A jacket torn, a silent plea,
Dismissed by those who refuse to see.

Yet, in the silence, a truth resonates,
A courage that injustice creates.
A vow to stand, to heal, to mend,
A promise to oneself, to ascend.

For though the system may turn a blind eye,
The spirit refuses to comply.
In the quiet, a power found,
A voice, once lost, now profound.

December whispers, ghosts reappear,
Messages from a past, once dear.
A haunting apology, empty and vain,
A reminder of a deep-seated pain.

Yet with each year, the spirit grows stronger,
Bound by the past no longer.
In the heart of winter's chill,
A resolve, a power, an indomitable will.

To reclaim the joy, the season's delight,
To banish the shadows, to embrace the light.
A journey of healing, step by step,
In memories kept, in tears wept.

A month that once brought fear and dread,
Now a path to tread, with cautious tread.
In the heart of winter, a flicker of hope,
A way to cope, to climb the slope.

Though the past may never fade away,
Strength is found in the light of day.
A determination to rewrite,
The narrative of the longest night.

Christmas, a time to reclaim,
To honor the journey, to acknowledge the pain.
In the glow of the holiday light,
A future, once again, bright.

A night that whispers still,
Of winter's chill and a will broken,
In a room where words unspoken
Echoed louder than the screams within.
A heart racing, a desperate din,
Against a backdrop of festive lights dim.

There, where trust was betrayed,
Where the lines of safety frayed,
A soul stood, fiercely unafraid,
Amidst the threats and shadows laid.
A battle of wills, a line drawn,
A spirit tested but never gone.

The aftermath, a silence loud,
A story buried beneath a shroud.
To the arms of law, a truth consigned,
Hoping for justice, for peace of mind.
Yet, met with disbelief, a cold shoulder,
The world, once warm, now seemed colder.

But resilience, a seed deeply sown,
In the face of dismissal, brightly shone.
A determination to move beyond,
To reclaim the self, of which one.s fond.

Seasons changed, yet one remains stolen,
A time of joy, now a reminder swollen
With memories of a night so bleak,
Of strength found when one seemed weak.
A ghost that haunts each festive cheer,
A shadow growing year by year.

Yet, in the telling, a power reclaimed,
A narrative owned, no longer shamed.
A hope that someday, Christmas will find,
A place in your heart, gentle and kind,
Where memories of shadows give way to light,
And the spirit of the season shines bright.

In the aftermath of a night so stark,
I found them there, in light and dark,
In a cafe corner, laughter shared,
As if the night's terror hadn't flared.

Jokes and coffee, a casual scene,
A stark contrast to where I'd been.
Abandoned, when I needed them most,
Left alone, a forsaken ghost.

The echo of betrayal, silent, deep,
A wound within, forever to keep.
For when the darkness closed in tight,
Those thought allies fled into the night.

In their absence, a lesson hard learned,
Of trust misplaced, of bridges burned.
A solitary figure in the fight,
A bearer of burdens into the night.

In solitude, a strength was found,
A resolve in silence, profound.
Though abandoned in my time of need,
From the ashes, determination freed.

A lesson in self-reliance, clear,
In the face of abandonment, a new frontier.
A path forward, alone to tread,
With the power of my own spirit led.

Reflecting now on paths since trod,
On the resilience, the strength, the facade.
Though once left to stand alone,
A greater fortitude has since been shown.

For in the journey from that night,
A self-discovery, a guiding light.
A realization of who.s truly there,
In the moments of despair.

The journey onward, marked by scars,
By nights under silent, watchful stars.
Yet, with each step, a reclaiming of self,
A putting of trust back on the shelf.

A recognition of worth within,
Beyond the betrayal, the hurt, the din.
A future envisioned, bright and clear,
Defined not by fear, but by the courage to steer.

In the aftermath of my silent screams,
Amidst the wreckage of shattered dreams,
A veil of silence, thick and dense,
A barrier, a false pretense.

My family, in their own way,
Chose to look the other way.
Failed attempts, a cry for aid,
Met with silence, debts unpaid.

But from the ashes of despair,
Emerged a will to repair,
To weave the broken strands of fate,
To rise above, to navigate.

In the quiet of my being, a wound resides,
A chasm deep, where silent pain abides.
Each year, as seasons shift and sway,
His specter returns, to my dismay.

With words that weave through digital threads,
He resurrects the memories, the dread.
A simple message, a note, a call,
Enough to make my fortress fall.

This wound, it bleeds with every word,
A pain so deep, it.s almost absurd.
A scar that refuses to heal,
With each contact, its sting I feel.

An endless cycle, a cruel game,
His apologies, always the same.
A tormentor masquerading as friend,
On his messages, my anguish depends.

Why does he reach through time.s thick veil,
When he knows his presence makes me pale?
Is it guilt, remorse, or cruel intent,
To remind me of the energy spent?

The trauma lives, breathes, and grows,
Fed by the past, it surely knows.
A never-ending echo in my mind,
A peace I search for but cannot find.

...Continues...

...Continued...

Yet, amidst the turmoil, a flicker of hope,
With this pain, I've learned to cope.
A resilience, forged in fire and strife,
Carving the path of my new life.

Though the wound may never fully close,
And his shadows linger, I suppose,
I am more than the scars I wear,
More than the memories we share.

I am a survivor, strong and true,
With each passing day, I renew.
For in the depth of enduring night,
I.ve found the courage, the will to fight.

Beneath the silent shroud of night,
When stars are dim and moon's soft light
Casts shadows long and spirits low,
My heart dreads the coming snow.

The world, in white, a canvas blank,
Each flake, a memory, a rank
In the army of the nights so sleepless,
Where dreams are few, and fears are ceaseless.

Snowflakes whisper, each a tale
Of winters past, when courage frail
Battled shadows, long and deep,
In the quest for just a night's sweet sleep.

Each flake, a specter, cold and bright,
Bringing memories to the fight,
A siege upon my peace of mind,
A battle, leaving rest behind.

The chill, it seeps through every seam,
Icy fingers in my dream,
A reminder of that fateful night,
When trust was broken, in snow's white light.

...Continues....

...Continued...

The silence of the falling snow,
A blanket over fears aglow,
In the quiet, my thoughts they race,
Through sleepless nights, I vainly chase.

Yet, in this battle, not all is lost,
Against the frost, my lines are crossed.
For within me burns a fire bright,
A will to claim the peace of night.

So, let the snowflakes fall and weave
Their chilly tapestries, I'll grieve
No more for sleepless nights they bring,
For in my heart, resilient, I sing.

A song of strength, of overcoming fears,
Of facing down the snowfront's tears.
With each flake that dares to fall,
I'll stand a little taller, I'll stand tall.

In the realm where trust was once a given,
Where guardians stood, by duty driven,
There lies a fracture, deep and wide,
A chasm formed from trust denied.

They, who were sworn to protect, to serve,
From this sacred path did they swerve.
In my hour of need, when I sought their aid,
My pleas for justice, lightly weighed.

The badge, a symbol of safety, of care,
Now a reminder of the despair,
Of a night when hope turned to dust,
In the hands of those I wished to trust.

With words dismissed, and fears belittled,
My faith in justice, cruelly whittled.
A system flawed, revealed its face,
In the shadows of my darkest place.

Now, when sirens wail in the distance,
I feel a surge of resistance.
A mistrust, deep-seated, and so keen,
For the protectors, not as they seem.

Yet, in this world of shadowed trust,
Where badges tarnish and promises rust,
I seek the light, however dim,
For healing, for strength, within.

...Continues...

...Continued...

A hope that from this pain, this strife,
Will emerge a trust, anew, in life.
In guardians lost, may we find,
A path to heal, to leave behind,

The mistrust sown in darkest hours,
To reclaim justice, to empower.
For in the end, it.s not too late,
For trust to mend, to navigate.

In the quiet corners of my troubled mind,
Where despair and pain are intertwined,
I reached for solace, for an end to the pain,
But found only shadows, again and again.

My cries for help, like whispers in the wind,
Unheard, unseen, by those kin,
My mom, my stepdad, faces turned away,
As if silence could make it all okay.

Beneath the rug, where secrets lie,
My pleas for help, my attempts to die.
Brushed aside, in the light of day,
A family facade, maintained in dismay.

Yet, in the silence of their disregard,
I found a flicker, a shard
Of hope, of strength, to carry on,
To face each night, each breaking dawn.

Shadows on the wall, in the dim light cast,
Echoes of my attempts, a haunting past.
A desperate search for an escape,
From a pain so deep, a soul.s landscape.

But in my home, where support should be,
A veil of silence, a refusal to see.
My struggles, my pain, merely brushed aside,
In their world, I must hide.

A rug that covers, not just the floor,
But my cries for help, my internal war.
Ignored, neglected, in my darkest hour,
Deprived of love.s healing power.

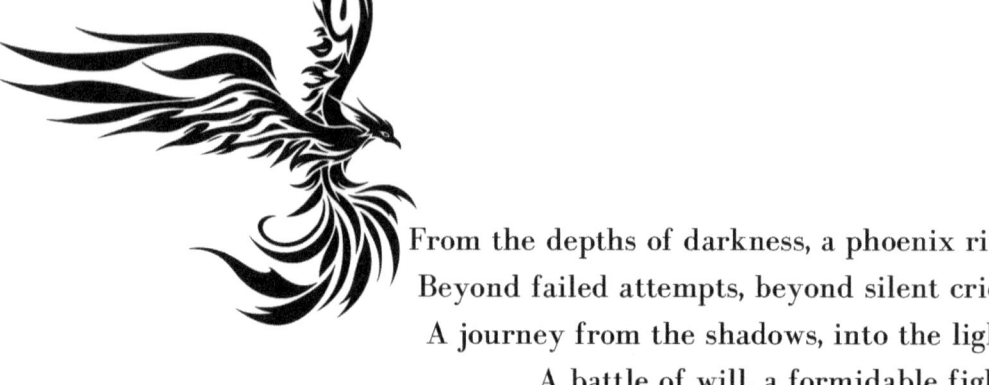

From the depths of darkness, a phoenix rise,
Beyond failed attempts, beyond silent cries.
A journey from the shadows, into the light,
A battle of will, a formidable fight.

Though brushed under the rug, my pain, my fear,
Within me, a resolve, crystal clear.
To live, to love, to find a way,
Despite the silence, to seize the day.

A testament to resilience, to strength unspoken,
A spirit unbowed, unbroken.
For in the face of neglect, of pain brushed aside,
Is a soul reborn, in dignity, pride.

In the silence of a home, echoes bound,
Where words of pain and fear resound.
From Oakville's warmth to Burlington's strain,
A journey marked by loss and gain.

A child's curiosity, flames set free,
A house, a home, no longer to be.
In grandmother's arms, a brief respite found,
Yet in new schools, old bullies abound.

With each move, a heart further torn,
A soul battered, weary, and worn.
In silence, anxiety and depression grew,
A family's disbelief, through and through.

A voice, unheard, in the vastness of night,
Struggling alone, fighting the fight.
Attempts to escape, unseen scars,
A family's gaze distant, like stars.

In the shadows of love unspoken,
A heart cries out, already broken.
Therapy's door opened, then closed,
A chapter of pain, prematurely composed.

A bus ride, a storm, a moment frozen in time,
A little girl's accident, a bell's mournful chime.
Rain's relentless pour, a soul's silent scream,
A life forever changed by a fleeting dream.

Anxiety's grip, tight on journeys anew,
On buses, in crowds, in everything I do.
Yet survival speaks of strength, quiet and deep,
A promise to oneself, forever to keep.

In the quietest hours of the night,
When stars are hidden from sight,
I hear the call, soft and clear,
From an old friend I once held dear.

A friend named Blade, cold and keen,
Whose whispers cut through what's unseen.
Promising solace, a moment's peace,
In exchange for a release.

My skin, a canvas, tells stories untold,
Of battles within, of nights so cold.
Each scar, an echo of a moment's pain,
A reminder of what I sought to gain.

But these marks, they do not define me,
They are but whispers of what used to be.
A testament to battles fought and won,
Underneath the moon and sun.

With every call, a dance begins,
A tango of despair that spins.
Blade, my partner, leads the way,
In a dance I wish not to sway.

Yet in the steps, a rhythm found,
A painful beat, a haunting sound.
A dance that leaves its mark, its stain,
In the pursuit of numbing the pain.

My skin, a canvas stretched across time,
Bearing the marks of a silent chime.
Each line, a story, a memory's trace,
A journey's map, etched upon my face.

This body, a vessel, imperfect, true,
Harbors tales of all I've been through.
Stretch marks, like rivers, course and weave,
Reminders of the life I conceive.

Though mirrors mock and eyes may stray,
My worth, these marks cannot sway.
A tapestry rich, with beauty rife,
Each imperfection, a badge of life.

In the quest for perfection, a battle rages,
Against the tide of societal cages.
A stomach that rebels, refuses to conform,
To the ideals that the world deems norm.

With every curve, a defiance loud,
A stand against the beauty crowd.
Yet in this rebellion, a struggle deep,
For acceptance, in this skin I keep.

Though waves of doubt may crash and roar,
This body's shore is worth much more.
A vessel of strength, of love, of might,
Bearing the scars of every fight.

In the twilight of my room, I stand,
Gazing at a reflection, a command.
To see beyond the surface, the skin,
To where true beauty dwells within.

Stretch marks, a stomach not quite flat,
In the grand scheme, what's there at that?
Yet, in the quiet, a voice so small,
Whispers of beauty, standing tall.

For isn't there more to this vessel, worn?
Than the battles with image, forlorn.
In every imperfection, a story bold,
Of resilience, of warmth in the cold.

In the quiet shadows of my mind,
A wish whispers, unkind,
To sever the parts of me I despise,
Underneath the moon's watchful eyes.

A blade of thought, sharp and keen,
Cuts through the flesh, the spaces between,
Dreaming to sculpt, to refine,
A silhouette that matches the one in my mind.

The fat, the flaws, each imperfection,
Subject to this harsh inspection.
A desire so visceral, so acute,
To uproot, to trim, to absolute.

Yet in this wish, a pain resides,
A battle within, where self-love hides.
For what is left when parts are taken,
But a soul, raw and shaken?

Would the removal of these parts I scorn,
Bring peace, or leave me more forlorn?
For each curve, each line, each mark I see,
Is a chapter of my unique story.

So though the wish to cut away lingers near,
I strive to look beyond the mirror's sneer.
To see the beauty in the being whole,
To heal the division within my soul.

...Continues...

...Continued...

For I am more than the sum of parts I hate,
More than a figure to cut, to berate.
A tapestry woven with love and strife,
Each thread a vital part of life.

In learning to embrace, not sever,
I find a peace that lasts forever.
A journey towards acceptance, a difficult fight,
Guided by the hope of self-love's light.

Chapter Four:

Without The Mask

With the mask now gone, and face to the sun,
I stand unguarded, my many battles won.
No longer hiding, no more disguise,
Embracing flaws, under open skies.

Each scar, each line, a story to tell,
Of battles fought, of moments I fell.
Yet, here I stand, in the light of day,
Proud of my journey, come what may.

For in my flaws, a beauty rare,
A strength forged in despair.
A courage found in darkest night,
Now shines forth in the brightest light.

So here I am, for the world to see,
A perfectly flawed, beautifully free.
No longer hidden, my soul takes flight,
In flaws, I find my might.

In the aftermath of darkest days,
When hope seemed lost in a bewildering maze,
It was not from where I expected to find,
But from my stepmom and dad, kindness entwined.

They stood as beacons, bright and true,
Guiding me through the pain I knew.
With open arms, and hearts so wide,
They walked beside me, stride by stride.

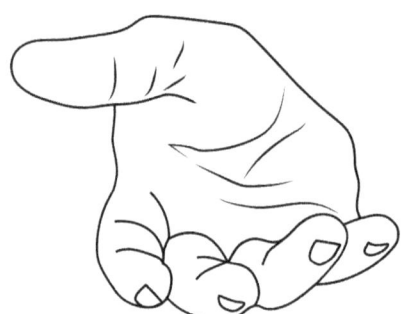 

From the depths where shadows play,
To the light of a clearer day,
My stepmom and dad, a steadfast pair,
Showed me unconditionally, how much they care.

In their eyes, no judgement found,
Only love and understanding abound.
They stitched the wounds of my battered soul,
Helping me, once again, to feel whole.

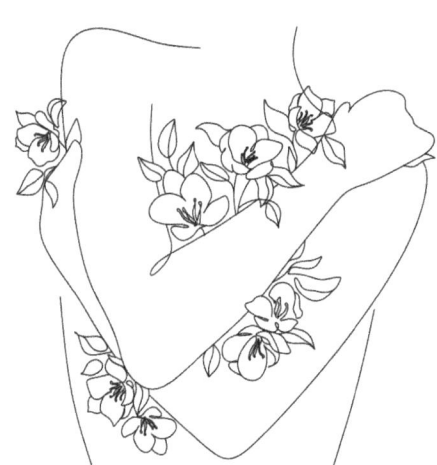

When life's storms raged, fierce and wild,
They stood unwavering, mild yet mild.
My stepmom and dad, my anchors firm,
Through every trial, through every term.

They did not brush my pain aside,
Instead, they were my guide,
Through conversations, tears, and healing,
They gave me back the feeling of feeling.

It was in their unwavering support I found,
A path to redemption, profound.
My stepmom and dad, in their grace,
Helped me find my place.

In their garden of care, I grew,
Learning strength, resilience anew.
For every tear, a lesson learned,
In their love, my life turned.

From the ashes of despair, a rebirth,
A new understanding of my own worth.
Thanks to my stepmom and dad's tireless love,
I found my wings, gifted from above.

In them, I found my haven, my light,
My reason to fight, to take flight.
Their love, a lighthouse in endless night,
Guiding me back, to what is right.

But time has taught me, day by day,
There are other paths, other ways.
To silence the call, to end the dance,
To give healing a fighting chance.

So to my old friend, I say goodbye,
With a heavy heart and a weary sigh.
For in the scars, I've come to see,
The strength to embrace a new decree.

Now, I march to a different beat,
One of hope, not of defeat.
The scars remain, but so does the will,
To heal, to grow, to climb the hill.

No longer does the blade call my name,
I've broken free from that old game.
In its place, a new friend found,
In the healing, in the sound.

Of laughter, love, and life anew,
A journey embarked, bold and true.
The scars, they whisper, but now I know,
They're just part of the story, part of the growth.

As the first rays of dawn kiss the sky,
So does the soul begin to fly.
Freed from the shadows of the night,
Embraced fully in the morning light.

No longer hidden, no longer shy,
The mask falls, the spirit flies.
Unveiled at last, the heart sings true,
In the unveiling, I find you.

Dancing freely, without disguise,
Each step a beat, under open skies.
The dance of the unmasked, wild and free,
A dance of one, a dance of me.

In the mirror, a new face appears,
Eyes unclouded by past fears.
Reflections unbound, finally seen,
The true self, calm and serene.

A road twisted, a road long,
Filled with right turns, filled with wrong.
Yet every step along the way,
Led me here, where I stand today.

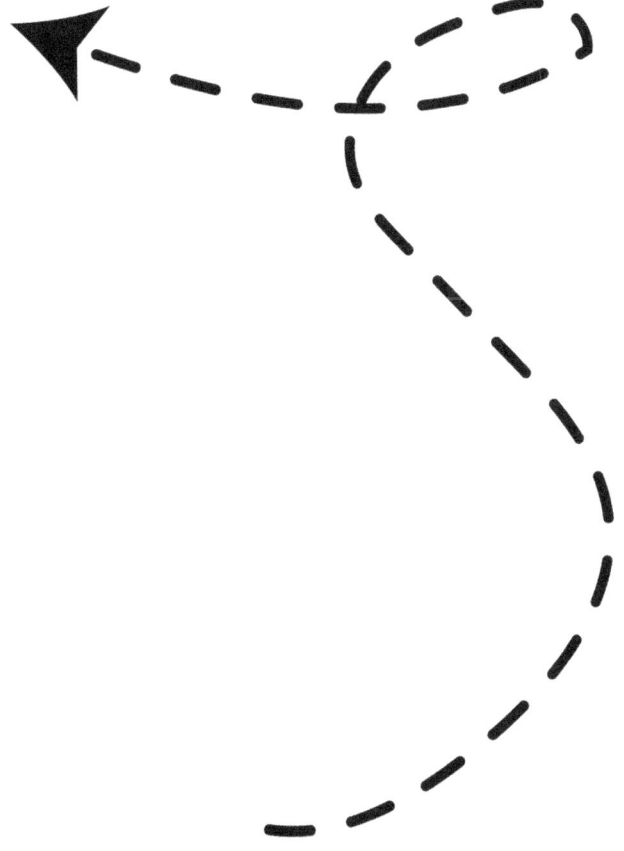

Like rivers carve the earth anew,
So does healing carve me and you.
Washing away the pain of the past,
Towards an ocean vast at last.

Listen closely, the heart whispers light,
In the quiet, it speaks of the night.
But also of the day, of love, of life,
Of overcoming struggle, of overcoming strife.

From the cracks, a flower blooms,
In spaces once filled with glooms.
Blossoming bright, against all odds,
A testament to the strength within, unflawed.

Walking barefoot, the ground beneath feels new,
Each step a declaration, brave and true.
A journey starts with a single pace,
Unmasked, seeking my own space.

I reclaim each piece, once given away,
Gathering myself, day by day.
In reclaiming, I find a power so vast,
A future unchained from the past.

Beneath the moon, unhidden, I stand,
No shadows to cover, no demands.
The moon.s gaze, a gentle embrace,
Illuminates my unmasked face.

Pages blank, waiting for the pen,
A story anew, begins just when
The mask falls, and the soul sees
Its unwritten chapter, a gentle breeze.

A rebirth, a renaissance deep within,
Shedding layers, letting new life begin.
The soul awakens, vibrant and whole,
In its renaissance, it finds its role.

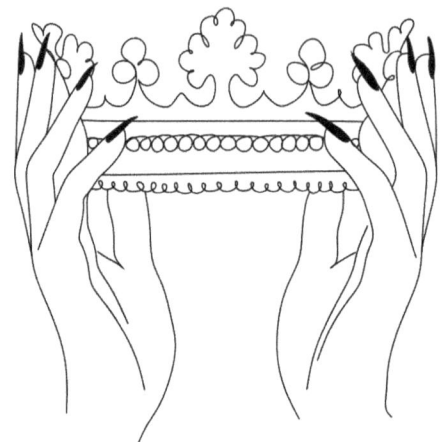

At last, the inner turmoil quiets down,
In its place, harmony.s song, a golden crown.
Singing of balance, of peace, of light,
A song of a soul, shining so bright.

Nurturing the garden within my heart,
Where once was barren, now art.
Flowers bloom, a colorful array,
In my garden, I choose to stay.

Eyes lifted skyward, I dare to dream,
Boundless, like the sky.s endless seam.
Unmasked, unbridled, utterly free,
Skyward, I find the key to me.

In the loom of time, threads intertwine,
Each color, each twist, a story mine.
Woven fabric, once taut and frayed,
Under the weight of masks portrayed.

In each thread, a lesson, a scar, a dream,
A tapestry of life, seam by seam.
Dark hues of trials, light shades of grace,
A portrait evolving, finding its place.

The weaver.s hands, steady and sure,
Embrace the flaws, making the art pure.
For in imperfection, beauty is found,
In the tapestry of self, I am unbound.

With every thread added, I see
The strength in vulnerability.
A masterpiece, uniquely my own,
In the tapestry of self, I have grown.

Beneath the mask, a world unseen,
A soul in shadows, a might-have-been.
Wandering through the fog of doubt,
A whisper of hope, a silent shout.

Through the valley of fear, I tread,
Carrying the stories, unsaid.
Each step, a battle, each breath, a war,
A fight to reach the distant shore.

But as the night gives way to day,
The fog lifts, revealing the way.
A path not easy, but clear and bright,
Leading me out of the endless night.

The journey long, the road rough,
Filled with moments, tough and tough.
But with each step, the burden lightens,
The soul heals, the horizon brightens.

For in the struggle, I found my might,
In the darkness, I discovered light.
A strength within, unbowed, unbroken,
By the words of truth, finally spoken.

No longer hidden, no longer scared,
My soul stands naked, fully bared.
The journey to the light, long and steep,
But worth every climb, every leap.

For at the end, what I found was me,
Unmasked, unguarded, finally free.
A soul reborn, in light, in love,
Journey to the light, a gift from above.

With roots deep in self-love, I stand,
Wings spread wide, across the land.
Grounded, yet free to fly,
Between the earth and the open sky.

In the stillness of dawn, a voice emerges, clear,
Not from the outside, but from a mirror, quite near.
A reflection now true, unobscured by the past,
Revealing a self, free from the mask at last.

This voice, it whispers of trials endured,
Of the silent screams and the battles obscured.
Yet, in its timbre, there's a notable shift,
A melody of liberation, so swift.

No longer a prisoner of expectations unmet,
Nor a dancer in shadows of a silhouette.
The chains of pretense, now broken, fall away,
Leaving a soul unbound, in the light of day.

A journey not simple, nor without its cost,
But in its undertaking, no true self is lost.
For in the echo of authenticity found,
Lies a harmony, profound.

A promise to oneself, to never again hide,
Behind the facades where true spirits reside.
For life is too fleeting, and love too vast,
To live in the shadows, or behind a mask.

Like a flower to the sun, I unfold,
Revealing stories yet untold.
In each petal, a chapter, a verse,
In this bloom, my universe.

There's a rebirth in the act of revelation,
A shedding of skins, a quiet celebration.
Where once there were layers, thick and worn,
Now stands a being, reborn and unshorn.

Gone are the veils that dimmed the light,
The protective cloaks that shrouded the night.
In their place, a figure, both vulnerable and strong,
Aware of where they.ve belonged all along.

This transformation, neither easy nor brief,
Challenges the heart, tests the belief.
But in this struggle, there's a priceless gain,
A peace with the self, a break from the pain.

The journey's written in lines of courage and grace,
In the map of laughter and tears on one's face.
Each mark, a story of love, loss, and fight,
A testament to the quest for what's right.

In this rebirth, there's no final end,
Just chapters anew, and wounds that mend.
A continual cycle of growth and of learning,
A fire of hope, forever burning.

Once, where shadows reigned supreme,
And hope was but a distant dream,
There came a light, fine and slight,
Through the cracks, breaking the night.

This light, a guide back to me,
To who I am, who I can be.
No longer hidden, no longer afraid,
In my truth, I am unswayed.

Through the cracks, the light it seeps,
Where the soul, quietly keeps
The essence of our truest form,
Now radiant, now reborn.

Here I stand, in my own sun,
The battles fought, the victories won.
No longer do I seek to hide,
In my light, I now reside.

Shadows may come, and shadows may go,
But in my sun, I find my glow.
A warmth that comes from deep within,
A strength to rise, a new begin.

Standing in my sun, I see
The power of authenticity.
A brilliance that's all my own,
In my light, I have grown.

No longer confined to the story once told,
I hold the pen, bold and bold.
The pages ahead, blank and wide,
Ready for the life I decide.

Unwritten, the future now lies,
Under the open, expansive skies.
Free to dream, to act, to be,
Unwritten, I am finally free.

Each step, each word, each choice is mine,
On this canvas, my soul to shine.
Unwritten, a path of my own making,
A journey of becoming, of unbreaking.

Like the ocean, change comes in waves,
Crashing over the life it saves.
Each wave, a force to be reckoned,
In its power, a lesson beckoned.

Embracing change, I ride the tide,
In its flow, I choose to glide.
For in the waves, I find my strength,
In their breadth, at length.

Change, once feared, now a friend,
On its currents, I ascend.
Riding waves of change, I see,
The endless possibilities of being free.

I returned to myself in quiet steps,
In the silent pact of secrets kept.
A reunion of heart, of soul, of mind,
In myself, my truth I did find.

A melody that's mine alone,
In this song, my spirit shown.
Notes of joy, of sorrow, of light,
In this music, my flight.

Beyond the fear, a world awaits,
Rich with love, devoid of hates.
Stepping out, the fear I shed,
Towards the love ahead, I tread.

No longer a prisoner of my own guise,
I see the world with new eyes.
With each breath, with each step, I see,
In my truth, I am finally free.

A new dawn breaks, clear and bright,
Chasing away the remnants of night.
In its light, I find my way,
Embracing fully the break of day.

At journey's end, a homecoming sweet,
Where self-acceptance and peace meet.
In my heart, a home I've found,
Within, where my true self is crowned.

As we turn the final page of "When the Mask Slips...", we find ourselves standing at the edge of a newfound understanding, gazing out at the horizon of our own becoming. This collection has been more than a series of poems; it has been a pilgrimage towards the heart of what it means to live authentically, unencumbered by the masks we wear.

Through the verses of vulnerability, the echoes of loneliness, the whispers of self-doubt, and the triumphant calls of acceptance, we've journeyed together. We've navigated the turbulent waters of revealing our true selves, confronting our fears, and ultimately, discovering the strength that lies in our fragility, the beauty in our imperfections.

This is not the end but a new beginning. The conclusion of this book is merely the first step into a broader world of self-discovery and acceptance. The masks we've slipped, the truths we've unveiled, are the seeds of a deeper connection with ourselves and with each other. They are invitations to continue exploring, to keep questioning, and to persist in our search for authenticity in a world that often demands conformity.

Let this collection be a beacon for those still navigating their paths, a reminder that you are not alone in your struggles. Your feelings are valid, your experiences are shared, and your quest for authenticity is noble and brave.

Your mental health matters. Your journey towards healing and acceptance is important. And in the moments of doubt, remember the essence of "When the Mask Slips...": that there is power in vulnerability, hope in the darkness, and an unbreakable strength in the courage to show your true face.

Thank you for sharing this journey with me. May you carry forward the light you've found within these pages into the world, illuminating your path and the paths of those you encounter along the way.

<u>Your mental health matters. Always.</u>

www.ingramcontent.com/pod-product-compliance
Lightning Source LLC
Chambersburg PA
CBHW052138070526
44585CB00017B/1877